The Body in Bioethics

WITHDRAWN

Recent debates about uses and abuses of the human body in medicine have highlighted the need for a thorough discussion of the ethics of the uses of bodies, both living and dead.

Thorough and comprehensive, this volume explores different views of the significance of the human body and contrasts those which regard it as a commodity or personal possession with those which stress its moral value as integral to the personal identity of individuals. *The Body in Bioethics* addresses a number of key questions including:

- Should it be legal to sell human organs for transplantation?
- Are public displays of plastinated bodies or public autopsies morally justifiable?
- Should there be restrictions on the uses of human tissue in teaching and research?
- Is the rapid increase in volume and range of cosmetic surgery a matter for moral concern?

This careful study of moral values provides essential background to many of the current controversies in medical ethics and is essential reading for all students of law, medical law and medical ethics.

Alastair V. Campbell is Professor Emeritus of Ethics in Medicine at the University of Bristol. He is founding editor of the *Journal of Medical Ethics*, a past President of the International Association of Bioethics and the author of ten books and numerous articles in the field. He is currently Chen Su Lan Centennial Chair in Medical Ethics at the National University of Singapore.

Biomedical Law and Ethics Library
Series Editor: Sheila A.M. McLean

Scientific and clinical advances, social and political developments and the impact of healthcare on our lives raise profound ethical and legal questions. Medical law and ethics have become central to our understanding of these problems, and are important tools for the analysis and resolution of problems – real or imagined.

In this series, scholars at the forefront of biomedical law and ethics contribute to the debates in this area, with accessible, thought-provoking, and sometimes controversial ideas. Each book in the series develops an independent hypothesis and argues cogently for a particular position. One of the major contributions of this series is the extent to which both law and ethics are utilised in the content of the books, and the shape of the series itself.

The books in this series are analytical, with a key target audience of lawyers, doctors, nurses, and the intelligent lay public.

Available titles:

Human Fertilisation and Embryology (2006)
Reproducing Regulation
Kirsty Horsey & Hazel Biggs

Intention and Causation in Medical Non-Killing (2006)
The Impact of Criminal Law Concepts on Euthanasia and Assisted Suicide
Glenys Williams

Impairment and Disability (2007)
Law and Ethics at the Beginning and End of Life
Sheila McLean & Laura Williamson

Bioethics and the Humanities (2007)
Attitudes and Perceptions
Robin Downie & Jane Macnaughton

Defending the Genetic Supermarket (2007)
The Law and Ethics of Selecting the Next Generation
Colin Gavaghan

The Harm Paradox (2007)
Tort Law and the Unwanted Child in an Era of Choice
Nicolette Priaulx

Assisted Dying (2007)
Reflections on the need for law reform
Sheila McLean

Medicine, Malpractice and Misapprehensions (2007)
Vivienne Harpwood

Euthanasia, Ethics and the Law (2007)
From Conflict to Compromise
Richard Huxtable

Best Interests of the Child in Healthcare (2007)
Sarah Elliston

Values in Medicine (2008)
The realities of clinical practice
Donald Evans

Forthcoming titles include:

Medicine, Law and the Public Interest
Communitarian Perspectives on Medical Law
J. Kenyon Mason and Graeme Laurie

Healthcare Research Ethics and Law
Regulation, Review and Responsibility
Hazel Biggs

Autonomy, Consent and the Law
Sheila McLean

About the Series Editor
Professor Sheila McLean is International Bar Association Professor of Law and Ethics in Medicine and Director of the Institute of Law and Ethics in Medicine at the University of Glasgow.

The Body in Bioethics

Alastair V. Campbell

Routledge·Cavendish
Taylor & Francis Group

LONDON AND NEW YORK

First published 2009
by Routledge-Cavendish
2 Park Square, Milton Park, Abingdon, Oxon OX14 4RN

Simultaneously published in the USA and Canada
by Routledge-Cavendish
270 Madison Avenue, New York, NY 10016

Routledge-Cavendish is an imprint of the Taylor & Francis Group, an informa business

Transferred to Digital Printing 2010

Typeset in Times New Roman by
Taylor & Francis Books

British Library Cataloguing in Publication Data
A catalogue record for this book is available from the British Library

Library of Congress Cataloging in Publication Data

ISBN 10: 1-84472-057-8 (hbk)
ISBN 10: 1-84472-056-X (pbk)
ISBN 10: 0-203-94041-5 (ebk)

ISBN 13: 978-1-84472-057-6 (hbk)
ISBN 13: 978-1-84472-056-9 (pbk)
ISBN 13: 978-0-203-94041-9 (ebk)

To Isla
For her gift of memories

Contents

Preface   **xi**
Acknowledgements   **xiii**

1 Why the body matters   **1**

Introduction 1
The ghost in the machine 2
The embodied self 4
Towards an embodied medicine 9

2 My body: property, commodity or gift?   **11**

The property paradigm 12
The commodification debate 16
The gift relationship 19
The value(s) of the body and its parts 23

3 Body futures   **27**

Flesh and blood 28
The organ trade debate 34
Contested solutions 48
Conclusion: which future? 53

4 The tissue trove   **55**

Property revisited 56
Humans eggs for research 63
Biobanks, altruism and trust 66
A common humanity 71

5   The branded body   **75**

The alien body   75
The ultimate fashion accessory   83
The fragility of beauty   89
Conclusion: the body and its discontents   92

6   Gifts from the dead   **95**

Dishonouring the dead   96
Gifts of knowledge   107
The gift of life   111
Gifts of memory   115

7   Together at last   **119**

Re-uniting the self   120
The lives of others   122
Earthbound   124

Notes   **127**
Bibliography   **133**
Index   **147**

Preface

Back in 2004, when Sheila McLean asked me to write a volume for her Bio-medical Law and Ethics Library series, I was happy to agree. I was shortly to retire (for a second time) from my Chair in Ethics in Medicine at Bristol University, and I foresaw a life as a scholar and a gentleman of leisure, with ample time to write. Not for the first time in my life, I misread the future entirely! Late in 2005 I was asked to apply for the newly founded Chen Su Lan Centennial Chair in Medical Ethics at the National University of Singapore. Over the past two years I have been involved full time in setting up a major new Centre in this international university, located in a vibrant Asian city. This has been a delight and a welcome new intellectual challenge – but hardly one that has left me much time for writing! However, the book is now written and it deals with an area in Bioethics about which I feel very strongly, not least because of my previous commitments in the UK, as Vice-Chair of the Retained Organs Commission and as Chair of the Ethics and Governance Council of UK Biobank. I would like to express my thanks to Sheila and the publishers for their understanding and forbearance, and for giving me the chance to write about a subject that has interested me for the whole of my professional life.

This book could not have been written without the outstanding assistance of my research staff, Jacqueline Chin and Voo Teck Chuan. Not only have they laboured many hours on the rather tedious tasks of summarizing sour-ces, reference tracing and reference checking, they have also provided many suggestions for new lines of investigation and have given me constant intel-lectual stimulus and support. I hope they are as fortunate in their junior colleagues when they reach my academic position. They, in turn, were helped in some of the research work by Gabrielle Bertier, a student intern from Paris, who managed to pack in an amazing amount of productive work in just a few weeks in the Centre, and by Jacqueline Chow. I would also like to thank several academic colleagues to whom I have turned for comment, insight or advice, in particular Nicola Peart and Leo de Castro, but also Peter Sykora, David Winikoff, Don Hill and Diana Teo. But, of course, all the infelicities of the arguments in this book are entirely my own.

Finally I want to thank my son, Michael, fellow philosopher, who shares with me the conviction that we need an ethics much richer than the thin gruel of Utilitarianism and the moral vacuity of Libertarianism, my son, Iain, whose passionate concern for the future of the earth has inspired the finale of the book, and my wife, Sally, without whose loving support and intellectual companionship this book would never have been finished.

Centre for Biomedical Ethics
Yong Loo Lin School of Medicine
National University of Singapore
August 2008

Acknowledgements

I wish to thank the *Journal of Medical Ethics* for permission to reproduce parts of the article 'They stole my baby's soul: narratives of embodiment and loss' by A. V. Campbell and M. Willis, *Medical Humanities*, 2005, 31(2): 101–4; and Hart Publishing for permission to reproduce parts of the article 'The ethical challenges of genetic databases: safeguarding altruism and trust' by A. V. Campbell, *King's Law Journal*, 2007, 18: 227–45.

Chapter 1

Why the body matters

Introduction

This book seeks to re-establish the importance of the human body in bioethics. But why is such a book necessary? Surely it is obvious that in medicine and in the human biological sciences the human body is of central importance! We need merely think of the worries about discrimination, breaches of privacy or loss of personal identity raised by the dramatic advances in cracking our personal genetic code, or of the powerful human need to overcome infertility that has led to an array of new technologies designed to achieve conception. Think further of the frustration with bodily deterioration, which fuels the search for pharmaceutical solutions to sexual dysfunction, cognitive losses and even the ageing process itself. Again, a modern obsession with bodily image has led to a move from 'cosmetic' surgery, initially developed to deal with severe disfigurement, to 'aesthetic' surgery, devoted to a reshaping of the body according to customer demand and the fashions of the day. Moreover, the centrality of the human body in biomedicine is nowhere more obvious than at the time of death. From a scientific perspective the human dead body – or 'cadaver' – is easily viewed in an impersonal way, as a source of knowledge of the causes of death or the effectiveness of therapy through autopsy, or as a source of benefit to others, through the 'harvesting' of organs and tissue. Such an objectified view of the dead body is, however, a universe of meaning removed from the perceptions of the bereaved family of a dead person. For them the body of the deceased represents all that they cared for and all they have lost. It was this disjunction between the scientific and the lay view of the dead body which led to the Retained Organs Controversy in the UK and in other countries. The depth of the horror felt by the bereaved relatives when they discovered that their child's organs had been retained without their knowledge or consent is well portrayed in this quotation from one of the government reports on the controversy:

> They were devastated to hear that their daughter's tongue had been retained, and the father protested silently outside Alder Hey ... They

describe the hospital as having stolen their daughter's body, which was 'white as driven snow'. It was reduced to skin and bone by predators and it must never happen again.

(Royal Liverpool Children's Inquiry 2001: 421)

The body, then, whether in life or death, is of central concern to most people's understanding of the moral issues raised by modern biomedicine and modern medical practice. Yet, strangely, it is either devalued or largely ignored in much contemporary writing about the ethical aspects of these disciplines. Reactions like those of the parents in the quotation have easily been dismissed as 'mere emotion', obscuring the real ethical issues entailed (Harris 2002). Bioethical writing tends to dismiss some adverse reactions to incursions on bodily integrity as no more than a 'yuk factor', stressing in contrast a 'rational' approach, which views the body as simply a vehicle for the self-aware rational moral agent. Once the person is dead, the body loses all significance in relation to that person, though others may remain emotionally attached to it. As we shall see, this evaluation of the relative insignificance of the body – the body merely as container for the mind, the true locus of personal value – accords very well with the dominant approach of modern scientific medicine. As a result, I shall argue that contemporary bioethics shares in the major intellectual flaws and moral deficits of this approach.

The ghost in the machine

To understand this problem adequately, we need to consider the philosophical assumptions that have led to this devaluation of the human body. Undoubtedly it stems from the revolution in thinking brought about by Rene Descartes, a seventeenth-century philosopher and physician, who can be seen as the father of modern scientific medicine, as well as the creator of a new philosophical method. Using his famous method of doubting all that could not be known with certainty, Descartes concluded that reality consisted of just two types of thing – *res extensa* and *res cogitans* – that which is extended in space and that which has no spatial location but which thinks. Mind and matter are thus two quite separate and distinct entities. Since the perceptions of matter mediated by the bodily senses are prone to error and illusion, the mind has access to the true nature of matter only through the pure operations of reason, represented by mathematics. When applied to the nature of the human person, this philosophy creates a radical separation between mind and body, viewing the latter as akin to a mechanism like a watch – the uniqueness of the person resides in the mind; the body is a mere container. This is a view of human nature usually described as Cartesian dualism, and it has been aptly summed up by the philosopher Gilbert Ryle as portraying the human person as a 'ghost in a machine' (1949: 15–16).

The power of this approach in creating modern scientific medicine cannot be underestimated. It desacralized the human body, allowing it to be studied as one would study any complex mechanism, without fear of this being an affront to human dignity and without need of divine sanction. Anatomical dissection was at the forefront of this new understanding of how the healthy body works and of the pathological factors which lead to disease and dysfunction. As the science of anatomy slowly freed itself from opposition by the Church and from its disreputable association with body snatching and murder (Richardson 1987), the foundations were laid for an empirically based medical practice, following scientific principles of investigation and testing out therapies by experimental methods, rather than by clinical anecdote and prejudice.

In his remarkable book *The Birth of the Clinic*, Michel Foucault (1975) describes the emergence of clinical medicine as the advent of a new kind of medical 'gaze' (*regard*), which 'sees' the disease beneath the visible surface of the human body. The scientific doctor has a special knowledge gained from the reading of clinical signs, whose meaning has been discovered by the science of pathology. Thus death has illuminated life. Foucault quotes the nineteenth-century pathologist Bichat: 'Open up a few corpses: you will dissipate at once the darkness that observation alone could not dissipate' (Foucault 1975: 146). Foucault comments: 'The whole dark underside of disease came to light, at the same time illuminating and eliminating itself like night' (1975: 195).

The legacy of Descartes can also be found in the way in which the philosophy of mind developed in the succeeding centuries. His method of doubt clearly influenced the British Empiricists, particularly Hume and Locke, who sought to identify the persistence of a rational and self-conscious agent, despite the vagaries of sense-experience. In the sphere of moral philosophy we find the Cartesian disjunction between body and mind repeated in Kant's elevation of the rational moral agent, who possesses a freedom of the will, immune to the distractions of bodily desire and emotion. In contemporary bioethical theory, there is a continuation of this tendency to elevate the (allegedly) rational and discount the bodily. Despite a rich variety of bioethical theories (Ashcroft *et al.* 2007; Brody 2003; Devettere 2000; Pellegrino and Thomasma 1993; Qiu 2004; Tong 1997), the dominant ones are the Principlist approach of Beauchamp and Childress (2009) and various forms of Consequentialism and Libertarianism, represented by Singer (1993) and Harris (1985). In these approaches, the Cartesian emphasis on a disembodied rational agent remains influential to a greater or lesser degree. For Principlism, moral judgments are made through applying four basic and universal moral principles, using 'reflective equilibrium' to solve problems of application or of apparent conflict of principles. For the consequentialists, moral dilemmas are solved through the dispassionate estimation of good or adverse consequences, seeking to reach a conclusion which any rational person could espouse. For this calculation to be truly rational there has to be a discounting of emotional factors (the often castigated 'yuk factor') and the discarding of prejudice (for example, the 'speciesism' which Singer (1995) believes contaminates many of our claims about the priority of human worth and dignity).[1] Libertarianism, stemming from a strong emphasis on Mill's assertion of individual liberty (Mill 1989; orig. pub. 1869), makes the choice of the individual paramount, unless clear evidence of harm to others can be proved. Although these approaches occupy a central place in contemporary bioethics, they certainly have not gone unchallenged. Notable criticisms have come from feminist bioethics in particular, where the insistence on a particular brand of dispassionate 'rationality' has been seen as yet another example of gendered discrimination, rejecting the more intuitive and relationship-based insights of feminist approaches to moral problems.[2] Nevertheless, debates about key issues in bioethics which affect the human body, such as the controversy over a potential market in human tissue and organs, still tend to be dominated by claims that it is irrational to treat the body with any special respect or to take any note of our intuitive repugnance at treating the body as an object of trade.[3]

The embodied self

What, then, might be a more adequate philosophical basis for understanding the significance of the body in bioethics? First, I must clear away a potential misunderstanding of my aim in seeking a revaluation of the place of the body in bioethical argument. I am not proposing to deny the centrality of reasoned discussion of ethical issues, nor am I proposing a return to pre-scientific medicine, casting aside all the obvious gains in understanding which have come from the objectification of the human body. My aim is, rather, to enrich our understanding of 'rational', by discarding the Cartesian disjunction between mind and body; and, at the same time, while recognizing the amazing achievements of scientific medicine, to see also its limitations in dealing with the patient as a whole person – as a union of body and mind. To gain this richer understanding we need to explore alternatives to the Cartesian disembodied mind, such as the 'mindful body' (Scheper-Hughes and Lock 1987), the 'lived body' (Merleau-Ponty 1962) or the 'embodied self' (Leder 1990).

We can begin our search for more adequate conceptualizations of the mind–body relationship in the writings of the neurobiologist Antonio Damasio. In two extensive explorations of the neurological roots of personal identity – *Descartes' Error* (1994) and *The Feeling of What Happens* (1999) – Damasio has mapped philosophical discussions of personal identity onto the latest findings about the structure and physiology of the brain. He convincingly demonstrates that attempts to separate the mind from the body are scientifically incoherent. His arguments are complex and extensive, but the essence of his account is captured in the opening chapters of the later work, *The Feeling of What Happens.* Here Damasio argues that the sense of enduring identity, which we experience in consciousness and build up through memory, is based on those basic structures of the brain which (nonconsciously) maintain bodily integrity. These structures ensure the survival of the organism against environmental pressure to assimilate it. Damasio writes:

> I have come to conclude that the organism, as represented inside its own brain, is a likely biological forerunner for what eventually becomes the elusive sense of self. The deep roots of the self, including the elaborate self, which encompasses identity and personhood, are to be found in the ensemble of brain devices which continuously and *nonconsciously* maintain the body state within the narrow range and relative stability required for survival.
>
> (Damasio 1999: 22)

Equally important for Damasio's account of the self are emotions, in their distinctively human form. In a powerful passage, which is worth quoting at length, he describes the significance of human emotion:

> At first glance there is nothing distinctively human about emotions, since it is clear that so many nonhuman creatures have emotions in abundance; and yet there is something quite distinctive about the way in which emotions have become connected to the complex ideas, values, principles and judgments that only humans can have, and in that con-nection lies our legitimate sense that human emotion is special. Human emotion is not just about sexual pleasures or the fear of snakes. It is also about the horror of witnessing suffering and about the satisfaction of seeing justice served; about delight at the sensuous smile of Jean Moreau or the thick beauty of words and ideas in Shakespeare's verse; about the world weary voice of Dietrich Fischer-Dieskau singing Bach's *Ich habe genug.*
>
> (Damasio 1999: 22)

Damasio's powerful description, written as a *neurophysiologist*, indicates how essential it is that we avoid the Cartesian disjunction between mind and body in describing our human nature. For the very core activities of self-consciousness and valuing, so central to rationalist accounts of the self, can be described adequately only if we see the inseparability of bodily based emotion from thought and judgment in ourselves and others. Of course, this is not to ignore the risk that emotions can prejudice our judgment, nor is it to subscribe to some kind of Humean notion that the reason is the 'slave of the passions' (Hume 1911: 127). The point is rather that a highly intellectualist account of what we mean by valuing in a moral sense simply does not accord with the way we are, as embodied selves, in which bodily experience and emotional response play a vital part.

Damasio points the way to a more adequate conceptualization of the mind–body relationship, but now we need to enrich the account by considering alternative philosophical approaches to Cartesian dualism. Here we can turn to the phenomenological school of philosophy represented by Husserl, Strauss, Merleau-Ponty, Foucault and others. In total contrast with Descartes' rejection of the reliability of sense-experience, phenomenology is based on descriptions of the world as perceived by the living subject. From these experiences, phenomenologists claim, the so-called objective world is constructed. We cannot reach some 'true reality' beyond that of the experiencing subject. All that we can know is the world that is constructed through the encounter of the self with that which is other than the self.

Starting from such a theoretical base we come to a total re-orientation of the mind–body relationship as portrayed by Descartes. Now what is basic is the 'lived body', and mental processes – what we call 'rationality' – are abstractions from the lived experience of our body. The radical implications of this re-orientation in thinking are well summarized by Shildrick and Mykitiuk:

> It is not simply that the binary of self and other is disrupted, but that the self, as a unified and identifiable entity, does not precede its own ... construction. In other words there is no sovereign subject, no central arbiter of truth or authority, no pre-existing agent of moral authority.
>
> (Shildrick and Mykitiuk 2005: 6)

Shildrick and Mykitiuk go on to discuss the loss of clear boundaries, which such rejection of the transcendent rational self entails. Embodied selves cannot keep themselves detached from the environment or from other embodied selves – they are inherently 'leaky, uncontained and uncontainable' (Shildrick and Mykitiuk 2005: 7). The rationalist's wish for a 'clean and proper body', enabling pure thought, is a myth. We cannot escape our corporeality, our fundamental and inescapable interconnectedness with other humans and with the environment we inhabit and construct.

The consequences of this re-orientation for ethics in general and bioethics in particular are clear. Shildrick describes bioethics as (literally) *out of touch* – it has sought to eschew bodily contact in favour of a supposed detached and impartial universalism. From a feminist perspective this can be explained in gendered terms. Maleness is seen as detachment from, and power over, the world. The male is dominant and in control – of the self and the other. Women by contrast are seen as emotional, overdependent on relationships with others, and with leaky bodies (menstruation being the prime example) which make them uncontrolled and unreliable. When translated into moral theory, these gendered valuations result in 'an ethics of autonomy ... of rights and interests, and of contracts; an ethics of fixed limits rather than an ethics of the lived and changing body' (Shildrick 1997: 215).

But can these radical re-conceptualizations coming from phenomenology, feminism and post-modernism provide us with a more satisfactory basis for bioethical theory than the anti-corporeal rationalism of Descartes? If we start from the lived body, from the embodied self, are we not cast adrift in a sea of relativity and subjectivism? Not *necessarily* so, but the task of creating a satisfying alternative account is a challenging one, given the huge influence of Cartesian rationalism on the way we have structured our moral discourse. To help me in this task I shall turn to one writer – Drew Leder – who has provided a comprehensive account of the relationship between phenomenology, medicine and bioethics, notably in his book *The Absent Body* (1990). I shall summarize his exposition of the embodied self, and then, in a concluding section, suggest in broad terms how it might be applied to the range of issues dealt with in the later chapters of this book.

Leder's descriptions stem from the insight that modern medicine takes as its basis not the living but the dead body: 'Modern medicine, profoundly Cartesian in spirit, has continued to use the corpse as a methodological tool and a regulatory ideal. Medical education begins with the cadaver, just as the clinical case ends with the pathoanatomical dissection' (1990: 146). But how can it happen that the lived body of the patient is so easily ignored? What is it that gives credence to the idea that the body is a mere animated machine, something different in kind from the individuality of the patient? Later in the chapter, I shall discuss how this mechanistic view has affected the practice of medicine itself, but first I must attempt to summarize a quite complex philosophical argument by Leder, which provides an explanation of how the lived body is so easily discarded or ignored.

Leder describes two aspects of our everyday experience which lead to this phenomenon – the *disappearing body* and the *'dysappearing' body*. Let us consider these in turn. The body constantly disappears from our conscious awareness as part of our normal waking experience. It does so in two forms: *focal disappearance* and *background disappearance*. First, *focal disappearance*: as we inhabit and move around the world using our powers of motility and perception, aspects of our body constantly appear and disappear from our awareness. Take an activity like riding a bicycle. If we have that ability, then our body co-ordinates eyes, hands and arms, muscles of our legs and feet, and the balance provided by our inner ear – all without any conscious attention to them. As our eyes seek out the route ahead we do not see the eyes themselves. Our eyes are not – and cannot be – part of our visual field. This focal disappearance is a basic characteristic of all perceptions. The organs of the body, which mediate the world, disappear from our awareness as they perform their function (we can look at our eyes in the mirror, but we do not see our eyes seeing the road ahead).

At the same time, as we cycle along, most of our body and its senses remain in the background, unheeded by us as we perform this task – this is *background disappearance*. We can, of course, bring these parts of our body into awareness, in a way that we cannot see our eyes seeing. For example, as we see a steep hill coming, we may shift attention to our hands to change gears or to our leg muscles in order to push harder; or, at the sound of a car approaching from behind, we may listen keenly to determine how close it is. But beyond these attainable realms of awareness, there are whole systems of our body, wholly essential to what we are doing as we ride the bike, but of which we can have no awareness at all. They are totally and irrevocably absent from consciousness. For example, we can be conscious – sometimes acutely conscious – of our breathing, of our heartbeat, or of our straining muscles as we cycle along, but those processes that oxygenate the blood or those which transform our breakfast into the energy that powers our limbs are entirely hidden from us. Moreover, while we have learned the co-ordinating skills that allow us to balance on two wheels and to steer a safe route through the traffic, we have no awareness whatsoever of the memory patterns, neural connections and feedback mechanisms that allow us to do that without thinking about it. This is the truly absent body – only perceived, as we shall see below, when it fails us. Yet all I know of myself and of the world depends also upon those aspects of my embodiment, which are totally outside of consciousness. As Leder neatly puts it: 'Reflective awareness rests on that which necessarily eludes it' (1990: 37).

We turn now to that second aspect of the body's absence, called by Leder the dys-appearing body ('dys', as in 'dysphonic', or 'dystopia'). He uses this term to convey those negative, jarring aspects of our bodily experience we encounter in pain and disease. As I mentioned above, we are not directly aware of the visceral processes that transform food into energy or of the cardiovascular processes that ensure delivery of oxygenated blood to the muscles and the brain. But when things go wrong with these systems, then the body occupies the centre of our consciousness, in a wholly negative way. We feel the pangs of hunger or the sharp pains of indigestion, a disabling faintness as our brain is starved of oxygen or the alarming warning signals of coronary arterial failure. In these dys-appearances, the body – rather than unobtrusively obeying the commands of our will – impedes it, or frustrates it altogether. Thus the body appears in the form of 'I cannot', at odds with what we want to do, or compelling us to do other things whether we want to or not. The body then becomes a stranger, even an enemy, rather than an ally, silently acquiescent in our chosen goals. Nowhere is this more clearly seen than in our mortality. Here the body, with its decreasing powers and failing senses, circumscribes our choices and finally puts an end to all our willed intentions.

If we now put together these two features of the lived body – its disappearances and hiddenness and its unwelcome frustrations of our intentions –

we can see how easily it can be both ignored and despised. In an influential part of the Western tradition, stretching back to Plato and given strong articulation in some forms of Christianity, the body has been seen as the prison house or tomb of the soul or spirit – *soma sema* (the body is a tomb).[4] The bodily desires become the seedbeds of sin and the senses deceive, concealing the true nature of reality. How much better, then, for our mind, or spirit, or soul, to cast itself free of the body and its distractions, in order to think clearly and dispassionately! But, of course, the paradox is that, without the body, we would have no locus of understanding in the brain, no powers of movement, allowing us the myriad perspectives we call the universe, no senses to mediate the shapes, textures, colours, sounds and odours of the only world we can even begin to know. Kant conveyed the dialectic of mind and bodily senses in a memorable saying: 'Concepts without percepts are empty; percepts without concepts are blind' (Kant 1965: 93; orig. pub. 1781).[5] In a more memorable analogy, he illustrated this interdependency by the image of a dove, which imagines how much faster it could fly without the resistance of the air – but of course, without the air it could not fly at all (Kant 1965: 47)!

Towards an embodied medicine

We have seen, then, how it has come about that modern medicine and modern bioethics can share in a kind of *folie à deux*, regarding the human body. Those hidden parts of the body and those pathological processes that cause pain and disease can be revealed by ignoring the lived body, by going below its surface once dead and revealing its structure and mechanisms in the dissected body. True, modern medicine, with its new imaging techniques, need not restrict itself to a corpse, but can gain amazing real-time pictures of physiological processes and of firing mechanisms in the synapses of the brain with the patient fully alive and conscious. But still the patient is inert, an object of study, and what is discovered by such observation must then be explained to her, like the map of some alien territory. She must be introduced, as it were, to her own body, as though to a stranger.

Playing in harmony with such a medicine of distance, bioethics tends to offer only de-personalized norms and principles, far removed from the patient's own narrative, cleansed of all particularity. Leder describes the consequences of all this for modern medical practice:

> The physician need not attend to the patient's intentionality when he or she is conceived of as a physiological machine ... Diagnosis and treatment seek to address the observed lesion, the quantified measurement, more than a person living in pain. The patient's own experience and subjective voice become inessential to the medical encounter.
>
> (Leder 1990: 147)

But is there an alternative? How could a proper acknowledgment of the embodied self lead to a more humane and genuinely therapeutic medicine, and to a bioethics that acknowledges the fullness of human nature, both mental and corporeal? In the rest of this book I shall try to give concrete answers to these questions by suggesting new ethical and policy implications of an embodied approach to medicine. Below I offer a brief sketch of what lies ahead.

In Chapter 2 I shall explore the contemporary debate about commodification of the human body, with specific reference to the question of whether, and in what sense, one can regard one's own body as property. Illustrating the issue with examples from current uses of human tissue, I shall revisit the idea of 'gifts to unnamed strangers' promoted by Richard Titmuss and relate this to the idea of honouring our body, derived from an account of the embodied self. This will provide the conceptual material for Chapters 3 and 4, which will deal with the controversy over blood and organ sales by live donors and the debate over what has been called the 'tissue economy'. In Chapter 5, I consider different ways in which images of the body influence people's behaviour, and I explore the social and moral implications of the rise of cosmetic or 'aesthetic' surgery. In Chapter 6, I move to the realm of the dead body, discussing both how we may be in danger of dishonouring the dead and how we may see them as sources of gifts to the living. In the final chapter (Chapter 7), I return to the question of developing an approach to medicine and bioethics 'beyond Descartes', suggesting that a more adequate account of our embodiment is not only personally and socially enriching, but actually crucial to human survival.

Chapter 2

My body
Property, commodity or gift?

The body has become big business. With the rapid expansion of transplantation of organs and tissues, the development of cell technology and the hope of ever new therapeutic marvels from targeted pharmaceuticals, the body and its parts have become of increasing interest to the health care industry. We have seen the emergence of what Andrews and Nelkin (2001) have called the 'body bazaar', in which all forms of human tissue gain commercial significance. At its extreme this bazaar is also bizarre, not to say macabre, reminiscent of the historical trade in dead bodies so well described by Ruth Richardson in *Death, Dissection and the Destitute* (1987). For example, just before Christmas 2005 it was discovered that the leg bones of the journalist Alistair Cooke had been removed from his corpse and sold for more than $7,000 to a company making dental implants (Waltz 2006; Scheper-Hughes 2006). Clearly the Cooke case is an extreme example, involving absence of consent, deception and (possibly) theft.[1] But what if there had been full consent by Cooke prior to his death and no deception? Would it be ethically acceptable for people to include as part of their legacy authorized sale of their bodily 'assets'? It could be their most valuable asset and could perhaps relieve the concerned dependents from destitution! And, if this would be acceptable after death, why not equally during life? Can we ethically view our body and its parts as a tradeable resource, to be removed and sold for financial gain, if we so choose?

This question needs to be resolved before we consider (in Chapter 3) debates about a market in human organs to meet the organ shortage or (in Chapter 4) the global market in human tissue fostered by the biotechnology industries. In what sense, if any, is my body also my property? And, if it is rightly so regarded, can it then be used as a tradeable asset of mine, akin to my other possessions, such as my house or my car? On the other hand, if we consider *trade* in bodies or their parts to be morally wrong, then we must explain why it is regarded as morally acceptable to *donate* them – what is the nature of the moral distinction here? These are the questions to be considered in this chapter, using as a moral guideline the concept of the embodied self expounded in Chapter 1.

The property paradigm

What do we mean by describing an object as property? We should note that there is no settled account of this concept, but rather a continuing debate between different types of explanation. Björkman and Hansson (2006) suggest that there are two basic approaches: a *natural rights* approach and a *social constructivist* approach. The former is classically represented by the philosopher John Locke. He argued that the earth was granted to all humankind by God – it was a *res communis*.[2] Individuals acquired property in this communal inheritance through the exercise of labour. This admixture of unclaimed material and human labour gave rights of individual ownership to the person expending the labour. An alternative view – the social constructivist approach – sees property rights as a social arrangement determined by the governing authorities to meet societally agreed goals, such as economic productivity or a fair distribution of resources. In this alternative view, there is nothing absolute or fixed about property rights. They can be decided, refined or altered according to what best meets the agreed social ends. An advantage of this second approach is that it allows for greater complexity and flexibility in what constitutes personal property. Rather than the assertion of some absolute 'natural right' to ownership – what Jeremy Bentham described as 'nonsense on stilts'[3] – we are left free to relate the concept of property to a more general understanding of the goals of society. Moreover, as circumstances change, it remains open to us to seek a revision in the way laws define certain objects as property. This is especially valuable in the rapidly expanding and diversifying possibilities for the use (or misuse) of bodily materials.

A bundle of rights

Pursuing further the social constructivist approach to property, we can now look at the bundle of rights and obligations, which ownership may encompass. A comprehensive list has been offered by Honoré (1961), comprising eleven types of legal relationships, which might be included in the description of an object as 'my property'. Honoré sees a 'family resemblance' between these eleven features, but does not suggest that all must apply in order for the term to be meaningfully used. Rather, the list provides us with a range of relationships between an object and its owner, which can be applied flexibly to a range of situations of ownership. The following is a brief summary of Honoré's list:

1 *The right to possess* – that is, to have exclusive physical control of the thing.
2 *The right to use.*
3 *The right to manage.*
4 *The right to income.*

5 *The right to capital* – that is, the right to alienate the possession by means of sale, mortgage or gift and the right to destroy it.
6 *The right to security* – the right to indefinite possession.
7 *Transmissibility* – the object can be passed on to the holder's successors or heirs, and so on indefinitely.
8 *Absence of term* – no time limit on the ownership.
9 *Duty to prevent harm* – either by owner's use of it or by use of it by others.
10 *Liability to execution* – the object possessed can legitimately be removed to settle a debt or deal with insolvency.
11 *Residuarity* – the object, if no longer owned by the possessor (for example if abandoned by him), may be owned by others.

This list may seem unduly complicated, and other simpler ones have been suggested. For example, the philosopher Sidgwick (1891) suggested just three features that constitute ownership – the right to exclusive use, the right to destroy and the right to alienate. However, the more complex descriptions of Honoré are illuminating for the discussion of whether the body or any of its parts may be appropriately regarded – *in some senses at least* – as property. Which parts of Honoré 's bundle seem appropriately attached to the body and its parts?

Let us consider first those parts of the list that *do* seem to apply appropriately to the relationship between me and my body. These are items 1, 2 and 3, relating to exclusive possession and use, and items 6, 8 and 9, relating to unlimited possession and my duty to prevent harm from use. It would be very odd to suppose that such rights and obligations, which apply to material property such as my home or my car, do not equally apply to my body and its parts.

But what of those rights which apply to transfer or removal of my property – transmissibility, liability to execution and residuarity? It is clear that while I am alive my body as a whole cannot be treated as capable of being removed from me (alienable) – I cannot transfer it to my heirs; I cannot abandon it, leaving it for others to gain possession; nor can it be removed from me in settlement of a debt. However, I can arrange for the removal and transfer of parts of my body, for example one of my kidneys or some of my blood, and these parts then become, in the senses noted above, property of the recipient (I cannot demand the return of the donated kidney, claiming it as still my property, once it is transplanted into another person). After my death, transfer of the body or its parts becomes even more viable. The law allows my next of kin to have 'lawful possession' of the body, though only for the purposes of proper disposal of it. Given adequate consents, parts of my dead body may be removed and transferred to the bodies of others – obvious examples being transplantable corneas and kidneys. Thus these items in Honoré's list do seem to apply, at least to some extent, to my body, in whole or in part.

However, the remaining items on the list, relating to income and capital, are the most contentious, since they equate the body and its parts with commodities, and it is here that the main disagreement about the status of the body as property arises. Given that Honoré allows a flexible view of the concept of property, we may be able to say that, in some senses, our bodies and their constituent parts *are* our property. But in reaching this conclusion, we do not in fact solve the moral problem at the heart of the debate about trade in body parts. To deal with this, we have to look more deeply at the concept of ownership as it relates to our embodied selves.

Limitations to the property paradigm

There are several reasons for seeing the language of property or ownership, when extended to include trading in body parts, as misleading and unhelpful morally. First, as we saw earlier, we do not 'possess' our whole living body as we might possess some other material thing, for example a set of clothes. We can remove our clothes, sell them, use them as barter for different items, give them to a charity shop or simply throw them away. None of this is possible in relation to our bodies, at least when we are alive (we can alienate parts of our body, but not our body as a whole). Indeed, as we argued in Chapter 1, there is no 'we' without our body. So, to alienate our body, we would have to alienate ourselves, for example through suicide or voluntary slavery. And there is a second problem in the concept of the body as our exclusive property. As Herring and Chau point out, 'Our bodies are not in any straightforward sense, "ours". They are interdependent, interconnected and intermingling with other bodies' (2007: 45). This is true from conception onwards. We are in constant dependency upon, and interaction with, the living environment, and from this relationship we gain life itself. This is at its most obvious in the fetal–maternal relationship during pregnancy, but it continues throughout our lives, right up to the moment of our death. The relationship between ourselves and the air we breathe, the food we ingest and the myriads of bacteria that help us convert that food into energy, is quite literally a vital one. Every moment of our lives is lived in (mostly unconscious) total dependency on our environment. Thus we are only in a very restricted sense separate beings. This is what Shildrick (1997) calls the 'leakiness' of our bodies.

Thus, it may be misleading to equate our relationship with our bodies to the relationship we have with our material possessions. As with all living beings, there is no watertight 'oursness' (as Herring and Chau (2007) put it) kept within the boundaries of our bodies – life constantly flows back and forward between ourselves, other selves and the environment in which we maintain our existence. Maintaining our bodily integrity within this state of dynamic interactiveness demands quite different procedures from those which help to defend us from trespass into our home or theft of our material possessions.

For this reason we may question the usefulness of those accounts of the body which seek to encompass it in the cluster of rights and obligations associated with property law. Given both our interconnectedness with others and the essential relationship between our selves and our own bodies (embodiment), it seems unlikely that an assertion of property rights over our body, of the kind we may hold over (say) a tract of land or a library of books, is the most effective way of defending ourselves against unlawful incursions into our personal space. Instead, we can surely rely on other types of human right, notably those which protect the privacy, dignity and inviolability of the individual person.[4] It is not clear what more is to be gained here by insisting on property language in respect of our bodies or the bodies of others.

A distinction between whole and parts

But, even if the body as a whole should not be seen as property, can we perhaps retain the concept to describe people's rights over parts of their body? For example, Lori Andrews, in an article (misleadingly) entitled 'My body, my property', seems to believe that we can safely distinguish between the whole and the parts:

> It is time to start acknowledging that people's body parts are their personal property. This is distinguishable from the past characterizations of people as property, which were immoral because they failed to take into account the nonbodily aspects of the individual ... and they created rights of ownership by others ... Allowing people to transfer and sell their own body parts, while protecting them from coercion, does not present these dangers.
>
> (Andrews 1986: 37)

A more nuanced account of this purported distinction between part and whole has been offered by Swain and Marusyk (1990). They suggest three levels at which the law could consider the status of human tissue. The first level is that of the whole body, and at this level all rights to possession and use are inalienable. The second level is that of 'a functional bodily unit such as blood, an organ, or cell, which can be transplanted into another person' (Swain and Marusyk 1990: 13). They argue that ownership is the wrong concept here, except to the extent that the parts could be held in trust, say by a hospital, wholly for the purpose of ensuring transplantation into another person. The hospital would have the obligations of a fiduciary relationship and could not treat these bodily parts as tradeable items. The third level – at which trade would be permissible – are products from human material, for example a cell line or a stem cell obtained from a cloned embryo, which comes from human material but is the product of human labour. The application of technology to the tissue would generate property rights in it.

A notable difference between the position of Andrews and that of Swain and Marusyk is that while Andrews wants to give property rights to the provider of bodily parts and tissues Swain and Marusyk explicitly prevent all claims to property in human parts or tissue, apart from when – in classical Lockean mode – labour has transformed their status. But then only the person employing the labour gains these rights. But now – one may reasonably ask – is this really fair? The classic case is that of Moore v. Regents of the University of California, in which a cell line was produced from cells in Moore's spleen but Moore himself was not accorded any rights to profits from that product of his own bodily part.[5] Such considerations take us to the other major issue in this chapter – the debate about the moral acceptability of treating body parts as tradeable commodities.

The commodification debate

Why shouldn't my body parts – or indeed my whole body after my death – be regarded as part of my (tradeable) property? After all, as Mahoney (2000) and others (Erin and Harris 2003; Steiner 2003/5; Waldby and Mitchell 2006) point out, many other parties benefit materially from human body parts – transplant surgeons, reproductive medicine providers, creators of cell lines, manufacturers of pharmaceuticals – so why should the tissue donor be excluded from financial reward? Is this not a hypocritical appeal to an altruism which only one party to the transaction is expected to adopt? Any answer to this question must deal with the central issue or whether, even if my body parts are – in some senses at least – my property, they are also correctly viewed as tradeable, that is, as commodities in a market.

Following Radin (1996) we can identify three features of objects which allow us to describe them appropriately as commodities: *alienability, fungibility* and *commensurability*. We have already referred to *alienability* above, when discussing the body as property. It describes my right to sell, mortgage, lease, give away or destroy all or any of my possessions (assuming, of course, that I am the sole owner of the object in question and that no other person has claim upon it). *Fungibility* refers to interchangeability in a market without loss of value to the owner. For example, I may choose to trade in my old car in order to purchase a newer model. Assuming that the deal seems fair to me, I do not regard the trading in as a loss of the value of the car. There is a straightforward equivalence between the prior value of the car when I owned it and its new value as part of the purchase price of the new car. *Commensurability* refers to the ability of objects to be ranked in value according to a common scale, most obviously money, though other ways of ranking may be found, for example equivalency of goods in kind. Taking these three features together, we can define commodities as those items which are appropriately regarded as having a market value. Of course market values are not fixed – they vary from time to time and society to society – but the *appropriateness* of the value of objects being described in market terms is the essential point. It is because they are rightly viewed as alienable, fungible and commensurable that objects are appropriately described as commodities.

It must be obvious from the above description – with its use of terms like 'appropriate' and 'rightly' – that I am writing evaluatively, not merely descriptively, about treating objects as commodities. Let us take an obvious example: it is a correct *description* to say that there has been (and probably still is) a market in slaves, just as there is ample evidence of a continuing market in child sex workers (ECPAT 2005; UNICEF 2005). However, the fact that vulnerable adults and children are *in fact* treated as commodities does not mean that it is *morally justifiable* to treat them in this way. On the contrary, it is a direct denial of human value to treat such persons as the possessions of others, as tradeable items whose value can be determined according to the going price in the market. This denial of value extends to persons treating themselves as commodities. Let us imagine a desperate father selling himself into slavery in order to raise enough money to feed his family, at least for a few months. While we may understand such a desperate move, it cannot be viewed as morally right, for a human person is not an alienable object which is fungible (interchangeable with other objects without loss of value) and commensurable with a monetary sum. Underlying this view of the moral wrongness of such commodification of persons is the dictum of Immanuel Kant that we should always treat moral agents, including ourselves, as ends in themselves, never as mere means.

But, assuming we grant this central moral principle about the moral wrongness of commodifying *persons*, does this prohibition extend to treating the (alienable) *parts of the bodies* of persons as commodities? Here we are in the realm of what Margaret Radin (1996) calls 'contested commodities'. She argues that there are currently powerful political and social forces leading us toward universal commodification of all aspects of persons, including their bodies. This derives from the pervasive influence of a free market philosophy, which in turn is based on 'negative freedom' (Berlin 1958) – the freedom to trade without interference from others or from the state. Radin believes that this assertion of negative freedom is self-defeating, for how can a person be regarded as free if at the same time she is regarded as no more than 'a manipulable object of monetizable value (from the point of view of others)' (1996: 56)? In opposition to this all-pervasive market ideology, Radin argues for a positive, not a negative, view of freedom – one which emphasizes the need for an enabling community in which the richness of total human flourishing is enhanced by non-market social structures. So, in opposition to the view that persons are merely traders in a 'free' market, Radin describes personhood in these terms:

> a better view of personhood should understand many kinds of parti-
> culars – one's politics, work, religion, family, love, sexuality, friendships,

altruism, experiences, wisdom, moral character, and personal attributes – as integral to the self. To understand any of these as monetizable or completely detachable from the person ... is to do violence to our deepest understanding of what it is to be human.

(Radin 1996: 56)

It is now time to consider how this discussion about limiting the scope of commodification relates to our topic – the viewing of body parts as commodities, items of trade in a market. Clearly our body parts – or at least some of them – are alienable, and indeed such alienation in the form of altruistic donation is actively encouraged for blood, gametes and transplantable organs. So if body parts are alienable in this morally justified way, then why should they not also be seen as tradeable – fungible and commensurable in monetary terms?

Wilkinson (2003) argues that opposition to the commodification of body parts has confused moral objections to the treating of *persons* as mere means to an end (the Kantian objection) with moral objections to treating their *bodies* as suitable objects for trade. According to Wilkinson such a view can be sustained only if we can 'make sense of the claim that persons (and *a fortiori* their bodies) are unique'. Since he can make no sense of this claim to uniqueness, he is 'left wondering whether commodification and fungibilisation are really independent wrongs or whether, instead, regarding persons as commodities is perturbing just because it's symptomatic of instrumentalisation, of regarding them solely as means' (Wilkinson 2003: 55).

We are faced here with a quite fundamental philosophical divide. Wilkinson's view represents what Radin describes as 'liberal compartmentalization'. This can be traced back to Kant's 'thin' account of persons solely as rational deciders. Radin writes: 'Kantian persons are essentially abstract, fungible units with identical capacity for moral reason and no concrete individuating characteristics. They are units of pure subjectivity acting in and upon the world of objects' (Radin 1996: 35).

The approach of this book, as will be evident from Chapter 1, is on the Radin side of this philosophical divide. The embodied self is very far removed from the Kantian abstraction of the rational will, and the uniqueness of individual persons, whose 'lived bodies' each have their own history, is a central feature of this approach. Thus we cannot brush aside concerns about commodification of the body and its parts merely by rejecting as meaningless claims about the uniqueness of individual persons. Perturbation about a trade in body parts relates to more than worries that it may be symptomatic of treating persons as mere means (though this, of course, is one aspect of our concern). It relates to a potential de-humanization of the self, by treating it as no more than a rational negotiator in a society dominated in all its aspects by market values, including the monetizing of parts of the human body. If we are to avoid such compartmentalization, then we need a 'thick' theory of the self. Radin describes this alternative view as follows:

when the self is understood expansively, so as to include not merely undifferentiated Kantian moral agency but also the person's particular endowments and attributes, and not merely those particular endowments and attributes, either, but also the specific things needed for the contextual aspect of personhood.

(Radin 1996: 60)

If we hold this richer view of the self we are bound to regard with concern attempts to treat all aspects of the individual, including the person's bodily parts, as readily detachable from the whole, as no more than tradeable items. At the end of this chapter, we shall return to the question of how market and non-market values might be related to one another in this complex area of the relationships between persons and their bodies. But first we need to discuss the related question of whether the alienation of parts of our bodies through gift can be regarded as morally different from selling them.

The gift relationship

To discuss the question we must turn first to the classic and highly influential work of Richard Titmuss, *The Gift Relationship*, and then explore the implications of his account for the debate about trading in body parts.

The essence of Titmuss's approach is captured in the subtitle of the book: *From Human Blood to Social Policy*. Although he is dealing with the question of whether the donation or the sale of human blood is (morally and socially) preferable, Titmuss draws broad conclusions from his study about the nature of altruism and human community. Titmuss is concerned with fundamental questions about the creation of an ideal human community in which the lives of all citizens are both protected and enriched. At the time when he was doing the research for the book he was concerned about the encroachment of a market philosophy into all aspects of social policy, including the provision of health care. For him, a society which fails to foster altruism and a real sense of communal responsibility and which fails to counter the natural human propensity for selfishness is doomed to moral failure and the collapse of humane social structures.

Acquisitiveness and greed, as he believed, will easily gain social dominance unless we create the kind of social arrangements that motivate us to care for others. The voluntary donation of blood is simply a powerful example of how altruism can be encouraged and the dangers of the market philosophy effectively countered.

The main research on which Titmuss's book is based is a comparison between the voluntary system of blood supply in England and Wales and the (predominantly) commercial system in the USA, although some reference is also made to other countries, including the Soviet Union and South Africa.

Titmuss's conclusions about the system of payment for blood in the USA are totally damning:

> From our study of the private market in blood in the United States we have concluded that the commercialization of blood and donor relationships represses the expression of altruism, erodes the sense of community, lowers scientific standards, limits both personal and professional freedoms ... legalizes hostility between doctor and patient, subjects critical areas of medicine to the laws of the marketplace, places immense social costs on those least able to bear them.
>
> (Titmuss 1970: 245)

Moreover (Titmuss adds), the commercial system is neither efficient nor safe – it wastes blood, creates shortages, is highly bureaucratized, raises prices and increases the likelihood of spreading disease through contaminated blood.

Giving to unnamed strangers

It is nearly four decades now since *The Gift Relationship* was first published, yet it remains a highly relevant and provocative work. In Chapter 3 I shall return to some of the detail of his arguments about efficiency and safety and to the criticisms that have been made of them, in terms of both their empirical claims and their theoretical assumptions. But at this stage I shall concentrate on what is arguably his central philosophical contention – that the voluntary donation of blood to 'unnamed strangers' helps to foster a sense of community and to promote altruism, in contrast with its commercial counterpart. Here we have the nub of a more general argument for distinguishing between the gift and sale of body parts on moral grounds.

David Archard, in a careful philosophical analysis of this aspect of Titmuss's argument, calls it the 'transformative claim' (2002: 89). In its negative aspect, it sees the market as having a contaminating effect on altruism; the market 'represses the expression of altruism, erodes the sense of community', to use Titmuss's words (1970: 245). This contaminating effect of the market could work in two ways. First, the *meaning* of my gift would be changed, since there is now a market price for blood. Rather than seeing it as the gift of life to a needy stranger, I now would see myself simply as making a financial contribution to the health service, waiving the financial claim I could have made for providing the blood. This would still be a gift, of course, but its meaning, according to this argument, is impoverished. Since blood is the stuff of life itself, to equate it to a financial sum is to denude it of its symbolic value. Second, now that blood has been given a financial value, my *motivation* to give would be removed, for why should I need to donate when hospitals can obtain commercially the blood required to care for patients? Further, why donate something, when I can sell it instead?

Thus, Titmuss argues, the market would diminish – or remove altogether – an invaluable communal effort, altruistic giving of blood to meet the needs of others.

Some writers have questioned the force of this negative claim. For example, Mack (1989) points to examples where a market price and a genuine gift easily co-exist. I may give my wife a sweater worth (say) $50 and also donate to my injured friend a pint of blood, whose market price might also be $50, but in both cases the gift is uncontaminated by the fact it has a market value. This is because it is not the monetary value that is crucial here, but my expression of love or concern for the recipient. However, this argument, as Archard points out, works only when *closely personal* relationships are involved (2002: 100–01). Of course, my wife and my friend perceive the value of the gift, not in monetary terms, but in terms of my careful choice of it, which demonstrates my appreciation of them as persons; and neither they, nor I, would see the value of the gift as diminished simply because it has a monetary equivalent. But these modifying features do not apply outside the sphere of such special, personal relationships. The whole point of Titmuss's argument is that my altruistic act expresses my sense of obligation to *strangers* (and to the community as a whole), and this sense of social responsibility and commitment to the welfare of others does not come naturally – it needs fostering (so Titmuss believes) by being clearly separated from commercial equivalents.

The positive counterpart of the gift relationship, according to Titmuss, is that it helps to build a caring community. But how convincing is this argument? One has to say that it would be hard either to prove or disprove it, for what measures would be the right ones to compare societies where commercial schemes exist with those where voluntary donation is the norm? It is obvious that a whole complex of historical, political and social factors will influence the ways in which communities are built up and maintained and the extent to which altruistic motivations are fostered. It is true that for many European countries 'solidarity' has been a key socio-political concept (Ashcroft *et al.* 2000) and that these countries also have a prohibition on the sale of blood and other body parts – but this hardly proves a causal relationship between the two! There are likely to be many ways in which altruism is fostered, for example by the growth of voluntary associations and charities, and the presence or absence of a voluntary blood donation system surely could not have the normative effect suggested by Titmuss.

How pure is the gift relationship?

Furthermore, the whole concept of the gift relationship, as expounded by Titmuss, needs closer theoretical scrutiny. Sykora (forthcoming) has criticized Titmuss's heavy reliance on the concept of gift, which he based on the work of various anthropologists, Mauss (1954), Malinowski (1922, 1926) and Levi-Strauss (1968). Sykora points out that the exchange of gifts, at least in the societies studied by these anthropologists, was by no means the opposite of commercial transactions. On the contrary, gift exchanges had a clear reciprocity, with the receiver of gifts under a strong obligation to give in return, and the size and appropriateness of gifts eliciting important social benefits (or disbenefits). Titmuss (as Sykora acknowledges) did clearly recognize the difference between the altruistic acts he was advocating and this traditional approach to gifts. For example, he observed that the donor of blood does not know the recipient of the gift, is under no obligation to donate and has no expectation of a direct return of benefit, as a result of the donation. Given these differences, Sykora argues that what Titmuss was actually advocating is much closer to the Christian ideal of charity (*charitas*, *agape* – loving your neighbour as yourself) than it is to gifts as normally understood. This may seem to be just a terminological distinction of no great importance. However, Sykora then goes on to argue that, rather than there being a radical distinction between charitable donation and sale, they are both in fact opposite poles of the same continuum, with gifts occupying an intermediate position between them. The common feature of all three is reciprocity, the difference lying in the nature of the exchange. The trader gets money or goods in exchange; the gift giver reinforces an important relationship; the charitable donor is rewarded with 'good feelings'. Here is how Sykora describes the continuum:

> On one pole of the continuum there is the pure altruistic donation of biological material, which is not reciprocated externally, however, it is reciprocated by experiencing 'good feelings'. On the opposing pole of the continuum there is human biological material as a commodity, which can be bought and sold. Between the poles there is a continuum of situations in which commercial and non-commercial practices are mixed together in various proportions, reflecting actual blurring of the borders between pure altruism and commerce.
>
> (Sykora forthcoming: 48)

The nature of altruism

So where have we got to in relation to the potential conflict between donation and sale of body parts? The key issue here seems to stem from our understanding of different kinds of transactions between people. Sykora's argument is that all such transactions, including allegedly altruistic ones, are based on reciprocity, even when the exchange does not involve the transfer of money or goods. There is, according to this analysis, no such thing as gratuitous social interactions – all have some reward for the donor, even though these may not be the obvious ones of financial, material or social gain. The argument is a fundamentally deterministic one: the assumption is that all human actions have causes of some kind, whether these be physical, psychological or social. Thus altruistic acts of giving to unnamed strangers must have some kind of sociobiological cause, possibly one related to the evolution of the human species and now built into our set of personal motivators. Titmuss's much prized gift relationship is in reality just a way of ensuring species survival, a socially useful curb on our more egoistic and destructive tendencies.

If Sykora is correct, then we need not pursue the gift-versus-sale debate any further. All that would need to be decided is what would be the more effective and useful social arrangements for obtaining body parts. This might turn out to be a combination of donation and sale, leveraging on the different motivations of different providers. The problem with such reductionist and deterministic arguments is that they offer no escape from the closed circle of their logic. If one starts with the assumption that all human actions can be fully explained through tracing the psychological and social determinants of individual behaviours, then any other reason offered for the way humans act must simply be translated into the same causal explanation. The only way to break the circle is to question the adequacy of the basic assumption. As I shall suggest below, this kind of deterministic argument works only if we take a monistic view of human values, one which depends ultimately on a consumer satisfaction model – your price for selling your kidney might be $10,000, but, because altruism is my motivator, my price is getting a surge of warm feeling about my higher motives.

Against such reductionist views, I would argue that altruistic giving reflects a completely different set of values from selling one's property. When you genuinely offer a gift to another person (known or unknown), you do not expect anything in return. Unlike selling or purchasing in a market, you do not calculate what advantage to yourself may come from the transaction. The recipient of the gift is not being treated as a means to your ends. Instead such genuine giving involves recognition of, and respect for, the needy other – even though that other is quite unknown to me. Thus the gift of blood, or of other needed tissue, such as gametes or a whole organ, perceives the importance of the life and goals of others and seeks to meet their needs. Of course, we *may in fact* use gifts manipulatively and as a way to gain advantage – commercial or otherwise – but it is surely integral to our understanding of altruistic or charitable giving that these are not gifts in a genuine sense. They are merely indirect forms of trading.

How then can we gain a more nuanced understanding of the relationships between gifts and sales of body parts? I shall seek to achieve this in the final sections of this chapter.

The value(s) of the body and its parts

Up to this point we seem to have been caught in a somewhat simplistic or unnuanced account of the controversy over the sale of body parts. Prohibitions of sale – such as those espoused by Titmuss in relation to blood supply – seem to regard the market as inevitably imperialistic and corrupting. Radin has referred to this view as the 'domino theory', and she summarizes it as follows:

> The domino theory assumes that for some things, the noncommodified version is morally preferable; it also assumes that the commodified and noncommodified versions of some interactions cannot coexist. To commodify some things is simply to preclude their noncommodified analogues from existing.
>
> (Radin 1996: 95)

We can see this approach in Titmuss's conviction that only through a voluntary scheme for blood donation can the social good of altruistic concern for strangers be fostered. In the opposite camp, advocates of a regulated market in body parts, like Wilkinson and Sykora, fail to see any inherent moral problem in conceiving of body parts as tradeable items like any other commodity. (They concede that *indirectly* wrongs may occur – for example through an unregulated, exploitative market – but these are not wrongs inherent in the commodification, but merely consequences of poor social control.) Supporters of a market in body parts, then, do not see any threat to personal values in treating them as fungible, commensurable with other objects and monetizable.

Is there a middle position between these two extremes? It seems important to find one, for the theories of Titmuss, as we have seen, make some unverifiable claims about the social effects of gifting, while the defenders of a market seem to see no problem in reducing the person to a rational trader inhabiting a potentially valuable piece of property. The middle ground may be found by recognizing, as Radin does, that no single value scheme can capture the complexity of our understanding of such intimate aspects of our lives as our bodily experiences, our relationships and our personal aspirations and commitments. We are here in the realm of what she calls 'contested commodities', a realm in which both market and non-market values can operate. The danger, however, is that – at least in today's intellectual climate – only market values will be perceived as the 'rational' ones. In *Value in Ethics and Economics* Elizabeth Anderson describes this problem as follows:

> According to the prevailing theory of value, people realize their good in having their wants satisfied. Markets are represented as generically appropriate vehicles for satisfying everyone's wants. According to prevailing theories of rationality, people act rationally when they maximize their 'utility' ... Market choices provide the paradigm for this kind of rationality ... so markets are presented as the generically rational form of human organization.
>
> (Anderson 1993: xii)

Both Radin and Anderson are seeking to offer, in opposition to this kind of reductionist and monistic account of values, a more nuanced account, in which we can recognize a plurality of values, all of which contribute to our understanding of ourselves as persons and our hopes for human flourishing and fulfilment. Anderson sums up her approach as follows:

> My theory emphasizes the richness and diversity of our concerns and finds a place for the full range of our responses to what we value. We don't respond to what we value merely with desire or pleasure, but with love, admiration, honour, respect, affection, and awe as well. This allows us to see how goods can be plural, how they can differ in kind or quality: they differ not only in *how much* we should value them, but in *how* we should value them.
>
> (Anderson 1993: xii–xiii)

Taking the more nuanced, pluralist approach of Radin and Anderson, I shall be arguing in the rest of this book that we need to avoid simplistic accounts of the value of the body and its parts. The position I shall be adopting in the various debates about the body in bioethics stems from a conviction that it is morally impoverishing to think about these issues without a full account of the nature of our embodied selves. This need not entail some kind of sacralization of the body, an inappropriate awe for what is, in the last analysis, merely the means to our existence as conscious, communicative and morally responsible beings. We can acknowledge that in many cultures – including Western developed societies – some parts of the body do acquire powerful symbolic significance, especially after the death of the person. (I shall explore this in greater depth in Chapter 6, when I discuss how a controversy erupted over the retention of human organs, notably the hearts of deceased children.) But we do not need to treat the body as a sacred object in order to pay heed to its importance. Instead, we need merely observe the obvious fact that all that holds ultimate significance for us – our intimacy with other persons, our appreciation of the beauty and complexity of the world we inhabit, our sense of ourselves as independent individuals, with hopes and fears, obligations and expectations which remain private to ourselves unless we choose to reveal them – all this, and much more that makes us perceive ourselves as human persons, depends upon our bodily existence. We may, of course, develop philosophical theories or religious beliefs that describe our significance in terms of free-floating pools of consciousness or eternal souls, for whom the body is merely a temporary resting place. But no such theory or belief can be formulated or communicated without the physical brain in which it was first formulated and the organs of perception by which it is communicated to others!

For these uncontestable reasons, the human body cannot be equated with the countless other material objects which ensure our survival, facilitate our communication with others or give us enjoyment. Terms like the 'dignity' of the human body have been suggested as a way of acknowledging its unique place among material objects. The use of this term has been criticized as confused and imprecise (see Macklin 2003, 2004; for a defence of the meaning and value of the concept of dignity in bioethics, see President's Council on Bioethics 2008), and it may be that the status it implies is higher than is appropriate. Nevertheless, we need to find a way of defending the body against those views which treat it as no different from any other exploitable material resource. The answer, I believe, will lie in making a value calculation in the various different contexts within which the body is potentially exploitable. If there is a common term to guide this discussion, then it probably has to be the term 'respect' for the body, despite all the vagueness also associated with this term! (I would see it as marginally better than 'dignity', since it allows for a change of status according to context, and it is such flexibility that I am seeking.)

In the chapters which follow, I shall try to ensure that we do justice to the richness and diversity of the values entailed in considering how we should view the human body in bioethics. I shall try to avoid global assertions about the moral rightness or wrongness of allowing trade in the human body and its parts, and instead discuss it in different contexts. For example, the diverse commercial and other uses of human cells and tissues in therapy, research and pharmaceutical product development present a real challenge to a simplistic opposition to trade, and instead require a realistic examination of 'tissue economies' (Waldby and Mitchell 2006). On the other hand, a market in blood and organs takes us into a different set of values, with greater personal, social and symbolic implications. The rise of 'aesthetic surgery' stimulated by powerful advertising and by an obsession in the media with 'ideal' bodily appearance requires separate discussion of the values involved. Finally, the treatment of the dead body and its parts brings us into another dimension of value, with powerful personal, social and symbolic resonances. The 'freedom' which the market is alleged to provide certainly needs radical questioning; but at the same time, we need to be sure that arguments for limiting the market's scope have genuinely rational foundations.

Chapter 3

Body futures

In a recent article in the *Journal of Human Rights*, Scheper-Hughes has written:

> how can a national government set a price on a healthy human being's body part without compromising essential democratic and ethical principles that guarantee the equal value of human lives? Any national regulatory system would have to compete with global black markets which establish the value of human organs based on consumer orientated prejudices, such that in today's kidney market an Indian kidney fetches as little as $1000, a Filipino kidney $1300, a Moldovan or Romanian kidney yields $2700, while a Turkish seller can command up to $10,000 and an urban Peruvian can receive as much as $30,000.
>
> (Scheper-Hughes 2003: 220)

The title of this chapter – 'Body futures' – reflects this inevitable implication of arguments in favour of the commodification of body parts. We live in a global market economy in which the 'sub-prime' mortgage crisis in the USA can result in a 'credit crunch' throughout the developed world. If people come to see their blood, organs or other body tissues as realizable financial assets, then logically they could become listed commodities on stock exchanges, with market forces determining monetary value within different economies (see Kluge 2000). My body and blood would then become (in a sense, literally!) part of my liquid assets. I could release the equity in them when I require the funds to meet my needs or desires. Just as the better off may release the equity in their homes to buy other things they need or want, so the homeless could release the equity in their bodies to *buy* a home (see Awaya *et al.* forthcoming).

Should we share Scheper-Hughes's condemnation of such a development as an assault on human rights, or should we see it as a quite reasonable respect for the autonomy of the poor to help themselves out of their poverty?[1] Or could there be a mediating position in which trade is avoided but some form of reimbursement or compensation is given to the donor? At this point, I shall consider this question only in relation to two possible items of trade – blood and transplantable organs – but in Chapter 4 I shall explore it more widely, by considering what have been aptly called 'tissue economies' (Waldby and Mitchell 2006), encompassing a much broader range of bodily tissues. I shall begin by discussing, in greater detail than in Chapter 2, the questions raised by Titmuss regarding the gift or sale of blood, and then, in the second part of the chapter, the current debate about gift or sale of organs from living donors.

Flesh and blood

To the biologist or medical scientist, blood is just another tissue, albeit a vital one for the body's functioning, maintenance and repair. But for lay people, across a range of cultures, blood is far more than that – it can symbolize regeneration and rebirth, kinship ('my own blood'), comradeship and commitment/loyalty ('blood oaths', 'blood brothers'),[2] vulnerability and sacrifice (death in battle, the Christian Eucharist, 'blood and sweat') or contagion ('bad blood', taboos against menstrual blood). (For further reading on the symbolic meaning and role of blood in human social life, see Meyer 2005.) It is hardly surprising, then, that donation of blood carries with it powerful overtones of unconditional care for others, that it is seen archetypically as the gift of life itself – as indeed it can be! There could be no more potent demonstration of this public perception of the power of blood than the upsurge in blood donation after the 9/11 attack in the USA. (Tragically, much of this blood was wasted because most of the victims did not survive, and the blood centres experienced a serious overload and a lack of subsequent donations (Dariotis *et al.* 2001).)

In Chapter 2, I summarized Richard Titmuss's description of unpaid blood donation as a potent example of 'gifts to unnamed strangers'. Titmuss believed this to be a key aspect of blood donation, since the gifting of blood both responded to and helped to maintain a sense of social solidarity. We shall return to this central philosophical point later, but first we need to consider the other arguments put forward by Titmuss in support of an unpaid system. These are related to the efficiency and effectiveness of the supply (including the minimization of waste), and the safety of the banked blood and blood products. Subsequent commentators have questioned these criticisms of the commercial system.

Efficiency and effectiveness

Titmuss published *The Gift Relationship* in 1970 and based his findings on studies carried out in the previous decade. According to Sykora (forthcoming), it is true that the American system at that time was poorly coordinated and inefficient, but this was due not to its commercial aspects, but to a complex mix of voluntary and paid systems of collection, leading to overall inefficiency. So far as wastage was concerned, recalculation of the data revealed that blood was wasted almost equally in the US and the British system (Schwartz 1999). There was also a change in demand in the decades following Titmuss's work, with a growing need for blood products for haemophiliacs, such as Factor VIII. This helped to expand the international commercial blood industry, since many European national blood transfusion services were unable to meet this need through voluntary, unpaid donation. Thus, European blood banks had to turn to the importation of blood products, sourced predominantly from American paid donors, despite the commitment in Europe to voluntary unpaid donation linked to the goal of self-sufficiency. By the end of the 1970s, the European blood market was a mixed public/private market system. Whole blood was sourced from local, voluntary, unpaid donors, and blood products from a mixture of voluntary unpaid and paid donors, from both inside and outside Europe.

We see, then, that the purely altruistic system envisaged by Titmuss turned out to entail some major problems on the supply side, especially in light of an ever-growing international demand for blood products. We turn now to the question of safety and comparisons between paid and unpaid sources.

Safety

Titmuss argued that commerce in blood procurement would impact on donor truthfulness/trustworthiness because of the profit motive and thus increase the risks of transfusion-transmitted infection. Moreover, payment for blood, he argued, would attract predominantly those who are economically disadvantaged and socially marginal, people who are more likely to be bearers of disease than the average members of the population. (This is known as the adverse selection problem: those who would readily sell you blood are precisely those you do not want to buy it from (Shearmur 2001: 30).) He drew empirical support for this argument by comparing the US and UK systems, showing a high rate of transfusion-transmitted hepatitis among those who received blood sourced from paid donors and a low rate among those who received blood sourced from voluntary, unpaid donors.

However, major scares about contaminated blood in the decades following Titmuss's work have made the debate more complex. The dichotomy between *gift*, and therefore good (pure) blood, and *sale*, and therefore bad (tainted/corrupted) blood, proved to be less clear with the advent of AIDS. The positive effects expected from using a pool of voluntary donors could easily be reversed by the presence of an infected donor in the group (possibly unaware of their disease status) and the negative effects of using a pool of paid donors could be addressed by quality control methods, like stricter donor screening procedures, more sophisticated testing and viral inactivation. Farrell (2006) points out the ambiguity, by comparing what happened in the UK and France following the advent of AIDS. After HIV testing became available, it was found that the UK had a comparatively low number of AIDS cases among blood transfusion recipients (whose transfusion source was from the local unpaid volunteer donor population) but a comparatively high rate of infection among haemophiliacs (who used blood factor concentrates sourced from American paid donors). France, on the other hand, had a comparatively high rate of infection in both blood transfusion recipients and haemophiliacs. In France the source of both blood and blood products was the local unpaid volunteer donor population, but these included some high-risk groups, including prison inmates.[3]

The conclusion to be drawn from these differences is that, since not all windows – the point of infection for a transmissible disease and the point at which tests will show positive results – can be fully closed, trust in donors (however well intentioned they are) cannot guarantee safety. A further illustration of this point comes from the emergence of variant Creutzfeldt–Jakob disease (vCJD), the human form of 'mad cow disease'. The incubation period for this disease can be very long, and currently there is no blood test available that can be used to identify someone who has been infected with vCJD. Some studies suggest that the disease is transmissible by blood, though there are uncertainties in estimating the degree of risk of infection through blood transfusion. Faced with these uncertainties, the British government decided to import plasma from American (paid) donors for use in the manufacture of factor concentrates to be administered to British haemophiliacs (see Weinberg *et al.* 2002: 317; O'Neill 2003).

In summary, the claims by Titmuss about the higher efficiency, effectiveness and safety of the unpaid system of blood donation are not incontestable. Predictions of consequences from paid versus unpaid systems will always have an element of unreliability, as circumstances continue to change and a rising demand for blood and blood products puts added strain on the voluntary system. For these reasons, Farrell argues that the dichotomy between paid and unpaid systems drawn by Titmuss becomes irrelevant, and could perhaps be a distraction from the real issues of concern. She writes:

> It [is] vital that other factors be taken into account in this regard, including institutional coordination of the blood supply on a national basis, epidemiological profiling of risks in the national donor population, an independent, well-resourced national regulator and a cost–benefit analysis of whether national self-sufficiency would in fact contribute to blood safety in the face of particular risks to the blood supply.
>
> (Farrell 2006: 168)

Nevertheless, it remains the case that a well-administered voluntary system can observe all of these safeguards, is likely to attract donors who have a less risky lifestyle and will be more likely to be scrupulous in testing than a commercialized system, since it does not have the temptation to compromise safety for profit.[4] For these reasons, as well as for reasons of principle (discussed further below), there is an international movement towards voluntary unpaid donation of blood. The World Health Organization (WHO), the International Federation of Red Cross and Red Crescent, and all the major international blood transfusion organizations now actively promote voluntary non-remunerated blood donation. Paid blood donation is being phased out in most countries worldwide as part of blood safety initiatives. Other than Bangladesh, most countries in the Asia-Pacific region have moved away from paid blood donation and toward voluntary non-remunerated blood donation as a sustainable safe source of blood supply. The biggest strides have been made in China, where the government put great efforts into reforming the blood system after the HIV scandals (Yu 2008). Today, voluntary blood donation makes up 95 per cent (2006 figures) of blood supply in China. Another example of rapid progress comes from Tanzania, with 20 per cent of donors in 2005 being unpaid compared with 80 per cent in 2007 (Brown 2008).

Nevertheless, the prospect for a safe and effective blood supply remains bleak for the majority of the world's population. Less than 45 per cent of donated blood worldwide is collected in developing and transitional countries, yet these make up 80 per cent of the world's population (WHO 2008a). The goal of 100 per cent voluntary unpaid blood donations, set by WHO in 1997, had been achieved by only 49 of the 124 countries surveyed in 2006.[5] Many of these countries still rely heavily on family/replacement donors and paid donors, both known to be less safe sources than regular donations from unpaid donors. Moreover, in these poorer countries the facilities for screening donors and blood may be either inadequate or absent altogether. Even when we look at a highly developed country like the USA, we find that, while *whole* blood donations are now entirely from unpaid sources, plasmapheresis donors are still paid. Thus the question of the safety of these products becomes crucial, especially since they are widely exported to meet the needs of other countries as well as of the USA. (A recent study of donors in the USA showed that donors who would be attracted by cash payments were 60 per cent more likely to be at risk of transmitting a disease (Glynn *et al.* 2003).)

We may conclude that, while it is true that unpaid voluntarism cannot *alone* guarantee an efficient and safe supply of blood products, it is a potent influence in achieving this, far superior to the uncertainties created by a market-based approach. To this extent at least, the claims made by Titmuss in the 1970s have surely been vindicated. (For a recent summary of this point, see Zimrin and Hess 2007: S16). But what of Titmuss's other claim, that selling blood undercuts key social values? We now return to this more contested aspect of Titmuss's arguments.

The in-principle argument

In Chapter 2 we noted the debate engendered by Titmuss's claim that a market in blood posed a serious threat to some fundamental social values. Thomas Murray summarizes the values at stake as follows:

> Gifts to strangers affirm the solidarity of the community over and above the depersonalizing, alienating forces of mass society and market relations. They signal that self-interest is not the only significant human motivation. And they express the moral belief that it is good to minister to fundamental human needs for food, health care, and shelter ... These universal needs irrevocably tie us together in a community of needs, with a shared desire to satisfy them, and see them satisfied in others.
>
> (Murray 1987: 35)

Similarly, Waldby and Mitchell describe the Titmuss view as countering social hierarchies based on income or status, since the gift of blood 'helps to constitute a sense of social responsibility and trust among strangers, and gratitude not towards particular persons but to the social body as a whole' (Waldby and Mitchell 2006: 16).[6]

Such claims were fiercely contested soon after the book was published, notably by Arrow (1972) and health economists Cooper and Culyer (1973). For these writers, the market was bound to be the best means of ensuring a good supply of a commodity for which there was a consistent demand. Inefficiencies and concerns for safety could be dealt with by better organization and by ensuring clear liability for defective products. One could not rely on the vagaries of altruistic motivation to ensure a supply, and, besides, those wanting to give rather than sell would still be free to do so. These arguments have a familiar ring at the present time, since they are now frequently used to promote a market in *organs*. It is notable, however, that advocates for a market in *blood* are now very hard to find! However, Shearmur (2001) has suggested one way in which altruism and the market might co-exist. He suggests that those needing to purchase blood and blood products to meet an escalating demand could turn to voluntary organizations, such as churches, where donors would be motivated by altruism and would be likely to be a safer source of blood. The donors of blood, he claims, would be expressing their altruism by benefiting their church through the income generated for the church by the sale of their free blood. In this schema, donating blood becomes a bit like passing on one's second hand clothes to a church jumble sale! But this description of altruism entirely misses the point of what Titmuss was seeking to promote. For him, the essence of altruism was that it did not single out specific persons or organizations with which one might have a special bond. Rather, it was an expression of care and concern for *unnamed strangers*. Thus it helped to create a society that was held together by more than contractual ties, or by ties of family or common causes. This kind of altruism is totally impartial in its scope, seeking to do no more than meet the needs of strangers. Thus, for the altruistic donor the act of giving blood is intrinsically valuable, not the means of raising money for a good cause, as it would be in a church fundraising blood donor campaign.

Embedded altruism

Healy's study (2000) of different blood collection regimes in Europe provides a more nuanced insight into the relationship between the motivation of individual donors and the systems used to collect, store and distribute blood. The study included thirteen countries, which were members of the European Union at that time. Donation rates varied widely, from as high as 44 per cent to as low as 14 per cent. The results of this study are complex and cannot be fully summarized here. But one significant finding was the effect of Red Cross involvement in ensuring a smaller, but committed group of regular donors. In countries with only a state-organized collection regime, a larger group of donors might be recruited, but they were less likely to give regularly. Thus, it was the powerful influence of the Red Cross, with its image as an international caring voluntary organization and its message about sharing the gift of life, as well as its highly efficient organization of the service, that achieved the desired result – a group of committed, regular blood donors. Healy concludes:

> Individuals may be moved to give their blood for any number of reasons, but it is the collection regimes that give individuals the chance to donate in the first place. Collection regimes embed altruism by creating opportunities to give. In the process they produce differing donor populations and show us that there is more than one way for a society to rely on the kindness of strangers.
>
> (Healy 2000: 1655).

This finding surely reinforces, but in a more detailed and empirically grounded way, the central point being made by Titmuss about creating and maintaining the 'freedom to give'. There is a two-way street between altruism and social structures; if we institutionalize unselfish giving by providing the structures that encourage and enhance it, then it will flourish; but if we try to replace it with markets, which rely solely on self-interest, then it will surely wither away. This conclusion clearly has relevance beyond the question of the organization of blood supplies, and I shall return to it, after considering next the ongoing debate about legalizing the sale of organs for transplantation.

The organ trade debate

Debate about the ethical appropriateness of a trade in human organs for transplantation shows no sign of abating at the present time. (As I was writing this chapter it erupted once more in Singapore, when the sellers, middlemen and intended purchaser of a kidney were arrested and charged under legislation criminalizing such activity. The subsequent debate in the press showed a strong, and almost equally divided, conflict of public opinion on the issue.) The question of payment or compensation for organs and the emergence of an international organ trade have led to new statements from WHO (2008b) and a conference organized by the Transplantation Society and the International Society of Nephrology, which led to the Declaration of Istanbul, published in *The Lancet* (Steering Committee of the Istanbul Summit 2008a). Later in this chapter I shall discuss these recent statements, but first we need to understand why this particular issue is so hotly debated and then explore the arguments for and against trading in human organs.

The organ 'crisis'

Since its development as a life-saving measure in the second half of the last century, organ transplantation has expanded exponentially, in terms of survival rates, the number of people on the waiting list for the procedure and the range of transplantable organs. Advances in immuno-suppression and in prevention of infection have led to improvement in the survival both of the recipients and of the transplanted organs. At the same time, there has been an increase in repeat transplantations (following failure of the graft) and in multiple organ transplants. The range of conditions for which transplantation is offered has widened, and transplantable organs now include: kidney, liver (or sections of liver), pancreas, heart and lung. Brain-dead donors can provide all of these organs, while kidney and sections of the liver and pancreas can also be obtained from living donors. Survival outcomes are better from living (related or unrelated) donors than from cadaveric donors, and, in the case of kidney failure, better from transplantation than from dialysis.

A consequence of this dramatic expansion in life-saving potentiality has been a worldwide demand for organs far exceeding their current availability, from either living or cadaveric sources. The following statistics illustrate why this situation is so frequently described as a 'crisis':

- In the United States today, there are almost a million people on the waiting list for all organ types (number of candidates: 99,111 as of 26 June 2008), with only 6,623 transplantations performed between January and March 2008. The number of registered donors does not exceed 3,374, including 1,401 living donors only. The median waiting time on the waiting list ranges from 38 days for the youngest recipients, to more than two years for the recipients above 50 years old. Nearly 20 people are estimated to die on the waiting list every day (United Network for Organ Sharing 2008).

- Within the European Union, 40,000 patients are registered on waiting lists, even though these have become more and more selective as an attempted response to the organ shortage crisis. Mortality rates range between 15 and 30 per cent, with more than 400 patients dying on the waiting list each year. Overall, only 12 per cent of European citizens possess a donor card, even though 81 per cent of Europeans are in favour of their use, highlighting a strong potential for improvement in the number of donors (Council of Europe 1999).
- In China, more than a million patients were estimated to require organ transplantation in 2000, with an average of only 13,000 transplantations conducted per year. Only 2000 kidneys are reported to be available for transplantation, but there are 100,000 people suffering from chronic kidney failure (Zhang *et al.* 2007).

Although significant efforts have been made in Europe and the United States to increase the number of donors and of successful transplantations, the organ shortage crisis is still evident, with what seems like a structural trend: demand higher than available organs. In the USA, a specific programme supported by the government – the 'organ donation breakthrough collaborative' – was implemented in 2003 to systemically identify, adapt and spread best practices associated with higher donation rates (US Department of Health and Human Services, Health Resources and Services Administration, Office of Special Programs, Division of Transplantation 2003). The latest report, gathering data collected from 1997 to 2006, shows that a significant increase in the number of consents, recoveries and successful transplants goes together with an increase in the rates of non-recovery and discarded organs (US Organ Procurement and Transplantation Network and the Scientific Registry of Transplant Recipients 2007). In other words, the volume increase has not been accompanied by a quality increase.

Scarcity scepticism

Given these dramatic statistics, it is hardly surprising that pressure is mounting to improve the quantity and quality of organs for transplant, and, since kidneys from living donors provide the best survival rates, some writers see it as an ethical imperative to introduce a commercial market to enrol more living kidney donors (Erin and Harris 2003). But, before considering the force of this argument, we need to consider why this particular health care problem attracts so much attention. There are, after all, many major unmet health care needs in the world today, despite the successes of modern medicine. Moreover, many of these are easily remediable and at much lower cost than the high-technology and very high-cost drug regimes entailed in organ transplantation. Obvious examples are malaria and HIV/AIDS transmission. (According to the WHO (2003), malaria and HIV cause more than 4 million deaths a year; in Africa, malaria is the 'leading cause of mortality in children under five years of age' while over 600,000 children were infected with HIV in 2003 alone.) Tragic though death from organ failure is, especially when it is the premature death of a young person, one needs to ask why it has become such a *cause célèbre*. Some writers have suggested that we need to be sceptical about the existence of this particular scarcity, since it is to a large extent created by false expectations about what medicine can deliver. Scheper-Hughes makes the point powerfully:

> The 'demand' for human organs, tissues, and body parts – and the desperate search among wealthy transplant patients to purchase them – is driven, above all, by the medical discourse on scarcity. The specter of long transplant 'waiting lists' – sometimes only virtual lists with little material basis in reality – has motivated and driven questionable practices of organ harvesting with blatant sales alongside 'compensated gifting', doctors acting as brokers, and fierce competition between public and private hospitals for patients of means. But the very idea of organ 'scarcity' is what Ivan Illich would call an artificially created need, invented by transplant technicians and dangled before the eyes of an ever-expanding sick, aging and dying population. The resulting artificially created organs scarcity is 'misrecognized' as a natural medical phenomenon.
>
> (Scheper-Hughes 2003: 206)

These observations about the false expectations of limitless medical progress and the injustice in meeting basic health needs which these create are clearly an important rebuttal of the idea that there is something *especially* morally scandalous about current failures to meet the demand for organs. It would seem that the transplant community has managed to promote its particular product to a privileged place of moral outrage (see the language used in Radcliffe-Richards *et al.* 1998 – 'denying treatment to the suffering and dying'; and in Erin and Harris 2003 – 'a major crisis and a major scandal'), allowing opponents of the market to be seen as cruel and inhumane, as well as prejudiced and irrational. Nevertheless, there are clearly genuine medical needs, common to both the developed and developing world, for which transplantation can at least be a partial answer. (A good example is to address the rising incidence of diabetes through better interventions and care management, given that diabetes has been shown to account for a higher risk of acute organ failure and associated mortality (see Slynkova *et al.* 2006).) We cannot dismiss the whole field of organ scarcity as mere hype, created by greedy health care professionals pandering to the illusions of wealthy patients. Moreover, whether we approve of it or not, the demand will not disappear, and it will continue to stimulate a market in organs, which in its present form is highly exploitative of the poor. As we shall see below, the market already exists – the only question is whether it could be transformed into an 'ethical market'.

Organ trafficking

There can be no doubt that, despite international condemnation and many national laws prohibiting it, organ trafficking exists in many parts of the world. A report prepared for WHO (Shimazono 2007) described the extent of the 'transplant tourism' taking place (so far as it could be ascertained, since getting a complete and accurate picture proved to be very difficult). I summarize the findings of this report below:

- First raised as early as 1985 by the transplantation society in the United States, 'transplant tourism' or the commercialization of organ transplantation, has now become a global industry, estimated to be worth more than $60 billion in 2006. Buying an organ from an anonymous donor living on the other side of the world becomes easier with the Internet, with several websites offering transplant all-inclusive packages. People mainly from Australia, Israel, Canada, the USA, Japan, Oman and Saudi Arabia travel abroad to receive a transplant from an anonymous live donor.
- The donors are often people living in severe poverty in third world countries such as Pakistan, India, Brazil or Bolivia; some are ready to sell their organs for as little as $1500. Most of the time, they are exploited by transplant middlemen, who promise them more money than they actually receive. They often engage in the process either to pay off debts, to be able to afford costly medical treatment or to buy land. They are very rarely given follow-up care, for financial reasons or due to discrimination, and are forced to start heavy manual work too soon after surgery. They often undergo chronic pain and fever, and complain of a significant deterioration of their health after the transplantation.

If this, then, is the current situation, is there not a moral imperative to find legal ways of meeting the worldwide demand, through a properly regulated market that protects both the vendors and the recipients, as well as increasing the supply of organs to meet the rising tide of organ failure? This turns out to be a very complex issue to resolve, with a whole range of arguments on both sides of the debate. Since live kidney donation has been the focus of attention in this debate, I shall restrict the discussion to that aspect of organ transplantation, though it should be noted that some of the arguments would apply also to other organs (part of the lungs, parts of the liver), as well as to post mortem organ retrieval (a topic dealt with in more detail in Chapter 6).

Commenting on the virtually universal ban on organ sales, Radcliffe-Richards *et al.* (1998) rightly claim that we need better reasons than feelings of repugnance for continuing the ban; most people will recognize in themselves the feelings of outrage and disgust that led to an outright ban on kidney sales, and such feelings typically have a force that seems to their possessors to need no further justification. Nevertheless, if we are to deny treatment to the suffering and dying, we need better reasons than our own feelings of disgust (Radcliffe-Richards *et al.* 1998: 1950).

However, this description of opposition to kidney sales as merely a 'yuk' factor seems like a caricature of the arguments usually made against legalizing a market. These arguments focus on some or all of the following factors: exploitation of, and harm to, the vulnerable; lack of genuine consent; loss of altruism and of donations from altruistic sources; and commodification of the body. I shall consider each in turn, with the arguments offered on both sides of the debate.

Exploitation

It is obvious that, in the present situation, the sellers of organs are the poor and the beneficiaries the rich. It is hard to imagine a market in which this would significantly change, unless the price were raised to a point where the better off were tempted to sell a kidney, but then how would such a market meet the evident need, since only the very rich would be in a position to obtain a transplant? Erin and Harris think that this problem could be resolved by creating a monopsony within a given region, e.g. the UK or the European Union, in which the central authority is the sole purchaser, the sellers and recipients are all citizens within the same geopolitical area, and allocation is made by the central authority 'according to some fair conception of medical priority' (Erin and Harris 2003: 137). However, the problems with such an 'ethical market' are that (as noted above) either the price would have to be very high to attract a range of sellers, thus escalating the overall cost of renal treatment and reducing its ability to meet the needs, or, in order to keep the costs reasonable, a price would be set that attracted only the poor into the market. (One could add to this the large administrative cost entailed in making sure such a market was genuinely restricted to those entitled to sell and to receive kidneys.) Thus it remains hard to see how the market can be organized in a way that does not inevitably make the poorer members of the society the source of the organs.

Several defenders of the market accept this consequence, but argue that this does not make the practice wrong. Radcliffe-Richards *et al.* (1998) use a lesser of two evils argument: even if there is some exploitation, this would be lessened by regulating rather than banning the trade, and, in any case, they argue, if people are so poor, surely any way of alleviating their poverty is better than closing that means of earning some desperately needed income. (I return below to the question of whether the trade does in fact materially benefit the poor.) Robert Veatch, in a recent (probably ironical) change in stance on organ trading, has used a similar argument, relating it to the failure to care for the poor in the USA. Pointing out that only the poor will find financial incentives irresistible, Veatch concludes, 'with shame and some bitterness', that paying the poor for their organs is the consequence of his country's refusal to help them out of poverty:

> If we are a society that deliberately and systematically turns its back on the poor, we must confess our indifference to the poor and lift the prohibition on the one means they have to address their problems themselves ... The time has come to admit defeat, join with the conservatives who have always accepted monetizing of the body, and legalize financial incentives to consent to procure organs from both cadaveric and living sources. [The poor] will no longer be donors, they will be vendors selling their bodies because the alternatives are all foreclosed to them.
>
> (Veatch 2003: 32)

Other writers, however, deny that a market which relies on the poor as sellers is necessarily exploitative. Wilkinson defines exploitation as '*unfairly* taking advantage of people's misfortunes' and he argues that, provided a minimum fee is set and enforced on traders in organs, using the poor as a source would not be unfair:

> Thus it seems hard to escape the conclusion that the setting up of a regulatory regime, which enforced a fairly generous minimum fee, not only would neutralize the exploitation argument, but may result in a considerable level of benefit for some of the poorest people in the world.
>
> (Wilkinson 2003: 131)

I shall return later to such claims about respective harms and benefits, but first we should note another type of argument countering claims of exploitation. This may be called the 'argument by extension', and it proceeds by comparing other ways in which we allow people to take risks in order to gain an income (coal mining, fire-fighting), or indeed to take risks just for pleasure, as in the pursuit of dangerous sports. So, Savulescu (2003) argues that if we are allowed to sell our labour, then we should be allowed to sell the means to that labour. If we are allowed to risk damaging our body for pleasure, why not risk damaging our body for other goods in life? Whether or not a market will increase supply or improve its quality, people have a right to sell a body part. To ban organ selling is 'paternalism in its worst form' (Savulescu 2003: 139). Another form of the argument by extension is found in Friedman (2006), in which a comparison with payment for participation on non-therapeutic research is used as a comparator:

Although most of these research protocols entail safe interventions, any investigation conducted to advance medicine and science may result in unexpected and even catastrophic events, as shown by recent cases in the US and UK. If it is reasonable, legal, and ethically justified to motivate someone using monetary reward to participate in human research, then by extension the same person should be allowed a monetary inducement or reward for donating an organ.

(Friedman 2006: 333)

Harm and benefit

How well do arguments about harm and benefit apply to kidney vendors? Is it true that the operation entails minimum risk, at least comparable to undertaking a risky occupation, engaging in a dangerous sport or enlisting in a drug trial? One difficulty is that we do not have good evidence of the long-term effects on kidney donors, even when these have been donated altruistically. According to Glannon (2008) it is likely that the risks over the longer term have been underestimated by health professionals. We do, however, know about the effects on participants of the currently illegal trade in organs. Goyal et al. (2002) reported the following findings from the trade in India:

- Among paid donors in India, selling a kidney does not lead to a long-term economic benefit and may be associated with a decline in health.
- Ninety-six per cent of participants sold their kidneys to pay off debts. The average amount received was $1070. Most of the money received was spent on debts, food and clothing. Average family income declined by one-third after nephrectomy and the number of participants living below the poverty line increased. Three-fourths of participants were still in debt at the time of the survey.
- About 86 per cent of participants reported deterioration in their health status after nephrectomy; 79 per cent would not recommend that others sell a kidney.

A more recent study of vendors in the Philippines by Awaya et al. (forthcoming) reveals a more complex picture. In this case 41 per cent of the 311 respondents reported an improvement in their finances, 17 per cent said there was no change and 36 per cent reported a deterioration. More than half of the sample would not recommend it to others, and health issues were of concern, with only 40 per cent returning for a medical check-up and 26 per cent reporting deteriorating health since the operation.

Of course, it may be that a regulated market could make a substantial difference to these poor outcomes for the vendors, but certainly claims by Radcliffe-Richards and Veatch that *merely by being vendors* poor people would improve their lot seem quite irresponsibly naïve.[7] Wilkinson does agree that the current unregulated system is exploitative, but seems to believe that the exploitation could be overcome by a 'fair' fee. This is woefully simplistic. First, he needs to make it clear who would determine this fee, on what basis of comparison it would be set and whether it would have to be varied depending on the economic status of a given country, as at present happens in the illegal market. (Of course, if this variation were allowed, then obviously the poorer nations would be targeted for the cheapest organs, a new version of 'sweated labour'.) Second, a fee alone is clearly far short of what is required to ensure the welfare of organ vendors. As we shall see later, international organizations have defined a whole set of conditions which would need to be met to ensure the long-term welfare of kidney donors. The alleged low risk of kidney removal is certainly very different when there is no adequate medical system to look after the donor after the operation and no system of compensation if things subsequently go wrong.

Supposing for a moment that a regulated market could iron out these problems of financial and health harms to the vendors, would comparisons with other risky choices then apply? Would having a kidney removed equate with the choice to engage in a risky occupation, to go on a skiing holiday or to be a paid research subject? Some writers have questioned the validity of these comparisons. Horrobin (2005) argues that risks in dangerous occupations and nephrectomy are not equivalent. Occupational risks are calculated over the long run, whereas the calculation of nephrectomy risks is based solely on the risks of the operation itself, and does not factor in the medical, social and psychological risks that continue to exist long after the surgery. Hence, a choice of facing a 0.1 per cent risk of death over working in something dangerous over the span of the employment is different from facing a 0.1 per cent risk of facing death during a nephrectomy operation. Joralemon and Cox write: 'admitting the exploitative and hence ethically objectionable nature of highly dangerous work conditions is not an argument for expanding the range of dangerous occupations or risky labour–body exchanges' (2003: 30). Annas (1984) points out that, if research is known to carry a high risk, then it is standard practice not to permit payments that would constitute inducements. It may be, then, that the arguments from extension are not particularly strong, and that Savulescu's castigation of the ban on organ sales as 'paternalism in its worst form' is misplaced. If part of the function of the law is to protect the vulnerable, then its use to prevent poor people from being induced to sell body parts to alleviate their dire financial situation could be seen as paternalism 'in its best form'. Consideration of this possibility leads us to the question of the nature of consent and its relationship to inducement.

Consent

It is widely accepted that there are three conditions for informed consent: competence, voluntariness and disclosure of adequately supplied and understood relevant information (see National Commission for the Protection of Human Subjects of Biomedical and Behavioral Research 1979; Faden and Beauchamp 1986). There is reason to suppose that two of these could be at least compromised in an organ market – voluntariness and adequate information. So far as information is concerned, one-third of the vendors studied by Awaya *et al.* (forthcoming) felt that they had not been given adequate information by the doctors and more than one-third did not receive any health counselling before consenting to the operation. Less than half of them went back for a medical check-up after the operation.

What about the voluntariness of the decision? Wilkinson (2003: Chs 6 and 7) argues strongly against the idea that the desperate plight of the poor, leading them to sell organs for whatever price is offered, constitutes a situation in which their consent is not voluntary and is therefore invalid. If desperate circumstances invalidate consent, he argues, then it would equally invalidate the consent of dying patients who seek treatment. Yet we believe that they make a reasonable and considered choice, despite their desperation. He also rejects the idea that an organ market is coercive, arguing that the coercion which invalidates consent has to be a direct threat of harm (or of an omission which would cause harm) by a specific agent. Using these criteria, Wilkinson can dismiss the coercion argument in the kidney trade on the grounds either that it does not apply, because no one person is directly responsible for the plight of the world's poor, or that it applies too widely, since it would have to be applied to *all* examples of the ways in which capitalism threatens the life and livelihood of the world's poor, not just to the organ trade. The problem in Wilkinson's arguments is well captured by Rothman:

> As … Amartya Sen has argued, economic development is too easily subverted by notions of a 'false liberty', the kind implicit in a so-called right to sell a kidney. Such practices deflect attention from and even undermine the structural changes that are vital to modernizing an economy. Sale of a kidney will no more rescue an individual from poverty than it will, in aggregate, spur economic development.
>
> (Rothman 2002: 1641)

Wilkinson is choosing to ignore the reality of the circumstances under which the organ traders find the vendors, measuring the whole thing against a Western notion of autonomy as freedom from constraints on my choices, what is often referred to as a thin account of autonomy (see O'Neill 2002). Here we have a prime example of what Benatar (2004) calls 'blinkered bioethics'. The circumstances of organ vendors are very different from the rational decider, free from direct threats, envisioned by his paradigm cases of voluntary choice. They are in fact targeted by kidney brokers because they are likely to be in debt already, and so likely to turn to whatever is offered to get clear of the threats of the money lenders (see Cohen 1999; see also the study by Awaya *et al.* (forthcoming), in which 91 per cent of the vendors gave poverty or finance related reasons for their decision to sell). The circumstances seem entirely different from the situation of a terminally ill patient faced with the choice of trying an experimental treatment or deciding to accept the likelihood of an early death. Either seems a reasonable choice, and many terminally ill patients in fact opt to receive only palliative care. This is not desperation in the same sense as it is for people for whom body parts turn out to be their only remaining asset.

I suggest, therefore, that at best we have to view the consent of organ vendors as seriously compromised, and that this puts a strong onus on those seeking organs from the poor to protect their welfare (a shift from a stress on autonomy to a stress on beneficence). Whether this can be done under market conditions is a point to which I shall return later in the chapter, but for the present we can describe them correctly as a vulnerable group, a description which may be paternalistic but is not necessarily demeaning.

The threat to altruism

We saw earlier in this chapter how the principle of voluntary unpaid donation has become the universal standard for blood banks worldwide. Why should this principle not also be universally applied to organ donation? Advocates for the market respond that this source has proved inadequate to meet the escalating demand for kidneys and other whole organs. (In fact this is not entirely true of all national situations, as we shall see in a later section of this chapter (pp. 51–3).) However, those who support an altruistic system argue that legitimizing a market in organs will undercut the voluntary system, since people who would have donated in the past would no longer do so if they knew there was a supply from the market. Some research has suggested that this could be the case. A study in the USA found that financial incentives would have an impact on only about 20 per cent of possible donors, and of these, while 12 per cent said they would be more likely to donate, 5 per cent would be less likely and the remainder were undecided (Kluge 2000: 282). A more recent study in Austria found a significantly negative effect on the intention to donate if financial incentives were introduced (Mayrhofer-Reinhartshuber *et al.* 2006). In Iran, following the introduction of a regulated market in living donations, there was a drop in cadaveric donation (Griffin 2007).

However, other writers have argued, on more theoretical grounds, that there is no reason in principle why altruistic giving cannot co-exist with at least some compensation, if not full payment, for donors. De Castro argues as follows:

> An organ donor gives much more than the physical organ that is transplanted to another body. The cost of the donor's participation far exceeds the cost that may be imputed to the physical body part. For this

reason it makes sense to talk about organ donation and altruism, even if the donor is given some form of compensation ...

When people are not compensated for donating organs to unrelated recipients, they are, as it were, forced to be altruistic. But altruism cannot be compelled.

(de Castro 2003: 145)

Others take this argument further still, arguing in effect that there is a moral duty to pay those who supply organs. So Erin and Harris speak of 'hypocrisy' in making the donor the only unpaid participant in the procedure:

There is a lot of hypocrisy about the ethics of buying and selling organs and indeed other body products and services – for example, surrogacy and gametes. What it usually means is that everyone is paid but the donor. The surgeons and medical team are paid, the transplant coordinator does not go unremunerated, and the recipient receives an important benefit in kind. Only the unfortunate and heroic donor is supposed to put up with the insult of no reward, to add to the injury of the operation.

(Erin and Harris 2003: 137)

There is, however, something rather odd about these arguments. In the case of de Castro's comment about 'forced altruism', it is of course correct to say that an act which is forced cannot be altruistic, since altruism is by definition the voluntary offering of help or care to another. But nobody compels people to donate their organs. This would be quite contrary to the whole concept of voluntary donation. Perhaps what de Castro had in mind was a family situation, where a relative might feel moral pressure to donate a kidney to a family member. It would certainly be wrong to press such a potential donor despite her hesitations, and if she did donate she should of course be compensated in terms of proper medical follow-up, at least. But this is not the situation that de Castro has in mind, since he speaks specifically of donations to unrelated recipients. Another interpretation of what de Castro means might be that people should be given proper social recognition for their altruistic act (as in recognition of blood donors through badges, ceremonies, etc.), or that they should not be *worse off* as a result of their donation, for example by losing their job or having their health compromised. However, though of course he sees these as important considerations (and very relevant in his own country, the Philippines, where the poor do not have adequate health care or social security), he clearly wants to go further than this, in terms of a regulated market, in which what he calls compensation would include some sort of payment, in recognition of what the donor has done. (He compares it with cash payments for information to the police, or to bonuses to teachers or other public workers for exceptional service.)[8]

This approach has sometimes been described as 'rewarded gifting', but as Murray (1992) and Veatch (2003) point out, this seems to be no more than a euphemism. It is clear that what is proposed is not an altruistic, voluntary, unpaid scheme in the normal meanings of those terms, but rather a form of regulated market. If this is so, then it is not correct to say that the *same person* can be both an altruistic donor and a paid donor, though of course one might have altruistic and compensated schemes running side by side. (But here the problem of discouraging the altruistic donation emerges again.)

The high moral tone about 'hypocrisy' and 'the unfortunate and heroic donor' adopted by Erin and Harris is even more surprising. Why is the donor 'unfortunate' if she has freely chosen to donate without financial reward? Perhaps the donor is 'heroic' in undergoing the 'injury' of surgery, yet advocates of the market like Erin and Harris stress the very low risk entailed! Most surprising of all is the attribution of hypocrisy. The hypocrite claims one thing but practises another (for example, he condemns homosexuality as a sin while practising it in secret). But transplant surgeons do not claim to be operating out of love alone whilst in fact taking fees! Nor do any of the other agencies involved in renal transplantation. Moreover, the organ donor is fully aware that she is participating in a paid, professional system – indeed, would surely prefer this, in order to be sure that standards were high – so there is no deception involved. What Erin and Harris may have in mind is the blatant profiteering associated with the current illegal trade in organs, in which it is well known that surgeons and middlemen make huge profits, with a tiny proportion paid to the vendors of the organs. This has nothing to do with the legal, voluntary system currently adopted in most countries in the world, especially those where there is a proper support and follow-up system for donors.

An analogy with donations to charity may help to make clear the irrelevance and mere rhetoric of the accusation of hypocrisy: if I donate to Oxfam in order to help the poor of the world, I do not expect workers for the charity to take no pay, nor do I expect the organization to compromise standards by employing people to carry out skilled work who do not have the necessary qualifications. Of course, if I suspect a charity is creaming off donations to make unauthorized and unjustified payments to its staff, or is misappropriating the funds in other ways, then I can accuse them of hypocrisy (and worse), and they must be brought to account. But the fact that there can be such dishonesty does not invalidate the appropriateness and fairness of using voluntary donations; and it certainly does not require that we introduce a paid system instead of a voluntary one. Thus Erin and Harris fail to make any valid case for the moral superiority of a paid system. (Were they correct, we would of course have to insist that the Red Cross start paying for blood right away, since they employ many professional health care staff, at normal salary rates.)

We can conclude that it is difficult to see how a voluntary and a paid system can co-exist without potential loss of organs from the voluntary source; and that there is no convincing argument to say that a paid system is in some sense morally superior or morally required. There may, however, be a moral case *against* the paid system (in addition to the fears of exploitation already discussed), and this concerns the issue of commodification of the human body.

Body commodification

Since I discussed the notion of commodification of body parts earlier (in Chapter 2), we need deal with it only briefly here. I summarize below the arguments which were discussed in more details in that chapter: in essence, the commodification argument against the sale of one's organs is that, although they are 'alienable' (I can have them removed from my body and transferred to another), they ought not to be regarded as 'fungible' or 'commensurable', that is, they ought not to be dealt with as though they were material objects whose value can be determined in a commodities market. To do so, it is argued, is to reduce one's body to a mere object, amongst other objects, failing to respect its special place as a part of my identity – my embodied self. So, in donating part of my body to help another, I make a personal investment in the other's welfare and survival; I give of myself to the other. But in treating my body merely as a means to income, I demean myself, through this instrumental use of my body parts.[9] This concept of the demeaning of the body through the organ trade is given strong expression by Scheper-Hughes:

> And the fetishized or 'designer' kidney purchased from a living donor conjures up primitive beliefs in human immortality, transcendence and magical energy. As Averham explained his frantic and dangerous search for a living kidney donor: 'I chose the better way. I was able to see my donor [in a small town in Eastern Europe]. My doctor pointed him out to me. He was young, strong, healthy – everything that I was hoping for!' Here, the symbolic equations between kidney market, slave market and brothel come to the surface.
>
> (Scheper-Hughes 2003: 214)

However, the equation of organ sales with lack of respect for the person has been seen by other writers as a confusion. Wilkinson (2000) argues that (1) there is no necessary connection between commodification of bodies and commodification of persons (consider X who buys an organ from a friend Y who needs some money; X may commodify the organ but not the friend Y); and (2) empirically, there is little reason to regard organ sale as worse in the commodification of persons than widely accepted practices such as buying and selling of labour (consider manual labour workers in some countries paid at the lowest possible rates by companies 'outsourcing' the manufacture of their brand name products). So if we are to prohibit organ sale, then we have to prohibit (at least some) of these widely accepted practices. In a similar vein, Gill and Sade (2002) argue that the Kantian opposition to treating persons as mere means can apply only to actions which would impair one's rationality and autonomy, and it cannot be that selling one's kidney impairs either of these.

A median position on this issue is taken by Radin (1996), who sees human organs as in the realm of 'contested commodities', where a case might be made either way for treating them on a par with other marketable objects. However, the danger, as she sees it, is what she describes as the 'domino theory', in which the prevailing culture of our age, which sees everything as monetizable, will steadily extend into realms hitherto seen as exempt from market value, thus eventually reducing the richness of persons to merely a set of marketable attributes. (This issue will arise again, in a different form, when in Chapter 5 I discuss the human body as the ultimate fashion accessory.)

Need we worry about such a creep from the instrumentalization of the body to the instrumentalization of the person if organ sales are legalized? Supporters of the market see no such danger, believing that a controlled and 'ethical' market will ensure greater respect for persons than the current illegal and exploitative organ trafficking. But an issue does arise, once we accept as a moral premise that there is no objection in principle to treating body parts as material assets of the person: on what basis do we draw a line in the authorization of the dismantling of the bodies of the poor to meet medical needs? Gill and Sade refer to this in relation to the possibility of heart transplants and point out (rightly) that the law could not authorize the killing of a person to provide a heart to another, but this is the wrong example. There are other body parts, without which a person can function (and be autonomous and rational), which are transplantable and needed for medical treatment. Examples would be people who seek replacement of a severed hand (an operation which has successfully been carried out – using hands from a cadaver – since the late 1990s (see Schuind et al. 2007))[10] and people who need corneal transplants (again commonly taken from cadaveric sources, though there have been accounts of people in Southeast Asia selling one eye to meet this market demand (Scheper-Hughes 2003: 198)).[11] We need to ask on what rational basis these sales can be opposed, once we accept that body parts are straightforward commodities. Thus the commodification argument against organ sales may well carry some force, not acknowledged by advocates of the market. For, on their premises, it is not clear why we would be entitled to legislate against the sale of *any* body parts from a living body, if they are not essential to survival or to cognitive functioning.

Contested solutions

How, then, is the crisis to be met in an ethical way? I shall begin by summarizing the basic principles, which have been recently re-affirmed by WHO (WHO 2008b) and endorsed in very similar terms by the Declaration of Istanbul, adopted by a meeting of the Transplantation Society and the International Society of Nephrology (Steering Committee of the Istanbul Summit 2008a).

The Istanbul Declaration makes an unequivocal stance against *organ trafficking, transplant commercialism and transplant tourism*. 'Transplant commercialism' is very broadly defined as 'a policy or practice in which an organ is treated as a commodity, including being bought or sold or used for material gain' (Steering Committee of the Istanbul Summit 2008a: 5). Clearly, then, the Declaration does not support in any way the concept of an ethical market in organs. The basis for this stance is spelled out in Article 6 of the Declaration:

> Organ trafficking and tourism violate the principles of equity, justice and respect for human dignity and should be prohibited. Because transplant commercialism targets impoverished and otherwise vulnerable donors, it leads inexorably to inequity and injustice and should be prohibited.
> (Steering Committee of the Istanbul Summit 2008b: 5)

This unequivocal stance is also found in the latest WHO document on the topic, in its Guiding Principle 5, which covers not only organ donation but also other tissue donations:

> Cells tissues and organs should only be donated freely, without any monetary payment or other reward of monetary value. Purchasing or offering to purchase, cells, tissues or organs for transplantation, or their sale by living persons or by the next of kin for deceased persons, should be banned.
> (World Health Organization 2008b: 4–5)

Both documents also agree this ban 'does not preclude reimbursing reasonable and verifiable expenses incurred by the donor, including loss of income' (WHO 2008b: 4), but they may differ slightly on the issue of insurance. The Istanbul Declaration requires the provision of disability, life and health insurance 'related to the donation event' (Steering Committee of the Istanbul Summit 2008b: 5) in countries in which such insurance is not universally provided. The WHO statement seems similar, but is clearly concerned to make sure that this is not a covert form of payment for the organ:

> incentives that encompass essential items which the donors would otherwise be unable to afford, such as medical care or health coverage

raise concerns. Access to the highest attainable standard of health is a fundamental right, not something to be purchased in exchange for body parts. However, free periodic medical assessments related to the donation and insurance for death or complications that arise from the donation may legitimately be provided to living donors.

(WHO 2008b: Commentary on Guiding Principle 5)

This difference in wording may not be particularly significant. Both documents oppose payments while supporting appropriate compensation. The WHO statement is perhaps clearer in its opposition to what is sometimes called 'rewarded gifting'. The socio-political reality is, of course, that those countries in which the current illegal trade flourishes are the least likely to be able to provide the kind of comprehensive care of donors which the statements require as a condition of allowing live donation at all. Thus, in effect, this international consensus on the subject is a powerful endorsement of the expansion and support of cadaveric donation in countries lacking a comprehensive health care system.

Let us now consider three examples of how, in practice, some national jurisdictions have sought to meet the demand for organs. The first is the only example in which payment for organs has been officially allowed (Iran); the other two provide examples of improved supply achieved without the use of financial incentives (Spain and Norway).

A legitimized market: Iran

Iran provides the only model of a legitimized market in organs from living donors, and this has led some commentators to use it as proof that an ethical and regulated market is possible and desirable. According to an editorial in the *Economist*, 'Governments should let people trade kidneys, not convict them for it' (16 November 2006). The scheme was put in place in the late 1980s by the Iranian government and it provides financial and insurance support to those unable to pay for organs from living unrelated donors, and allows payment to these donors. (The cadaveric scheme does not entail any payments apart from possibly funeral expenses for donor families.) As one might expect, with such a scheme in place Iran has the highest percentage of living unrelated kidney donations in the world, at 76 per cent, compared with less than 1 per cent in the USA and less than 10 per cent in the UK (see Griffin 2007; National Health Service 2007). The main features of the Iranian scheme are as follows (see Ghods and Savaj 2006; Griffin 2007):

- The Dialysis and Transplant Patients Association (DATPA), a non-governmental organization, acts as the regulative agency; no other agencies or brokers are allowed.

- The living unrelated donor receives a payment (about US$1200) from the government and one year's free health care.
- In addition the donor is allowed to receive a negotiated payment from the recipient. The DATPA arranges a meeting between the donor and the recipient, but does not set the amount of the payment. No records of the amounts paid are kept. DATPA may act as a guarantor of this payment by holding onto the money until the transplantation is completed.
- Costs of the operation are paid through a combination of the recipient's insurance and a government subsidy. Poor recipients are provided with government subsidized insurance and charities may assist them with the additional negotiated payment to the recipient.
- Foreigners are not allowed to donate, though they can receive a transplant, but *only if* donor and recipient are from the same nationality.
- The majority of donors are the poor (84 per cent) but the majority of recipients are also the poor (50.4 per cent). However, the measure of poverty may be too widely drawn (see below).
- Supporters of the scheme claim the following good outcomes: elimination of the waiting list for kidneys; removal of coercive (familial) pressures on living donors; prevention of transplant tourism in Iran; and prevention of Iranian patients seeking commercial or illegal paid transplants abroad.

So does the Iranian scheme provide a workable model, which could be adapted and applied elsewhere? A recent paper in the *British Medical Journal* (Griffin 2007), summarizing studies of the actual workings of the scheme, raises a number of doubts about its alleged benefits. First, the claim that Iran has *eliminated* its waiting list for transplantation now appears to have been withdrawn by the proponents of the system (Ghods and Savaj 2006), who have admitted that many patients from rural areas are not diagnosed and so are not referred for dialysis, and thus are not put on a waiting list for transplantation. Other commentators have pointed out that many people may not be able to afford the living donor programme (despite the various subsidies) and so are in fact on a waiting list for *cadaveric* kidneys, which do not entail the same costs, but for which there is a significant waiting time. Others are simply not scheduled for transplantation (Broumand 2005). Some research suggests that women and the unemployed are less likely to be listed (Griffin 2007).

Second, the claim that the organs are given to the poor as well as taken from the poor (Ghods *et al.* 2001) is based on a very broad definition of 'poverty', as unable 'to afford average housing and food and college training for children'. Griffin points out that the reality is that the donors are likely to be in more desperate straits than those able to afford below average housing.

Third, it is widely acknowledged that the system of paid live donation has undermined the other potential sources of donation in Iran: altruistic donation from family members and cadaveric donation. The latter is still dramatically low in Iran compared with other parts of the world (1.8 per million population in 2006, compared with 26.9 for the USA and 10.5 for the UK (Sanz *et al.* 2007)). As we shall see when we discuss the situation in Norway and Spain, these alternative sources can yield very good results and they do not entail the ethical pitfalls of the paid system.

Finally, it is not in fact true that the market is regulated in Iran. Although the government fixes the amount of the standard payment (as well as providing free health care in a country which lacks universal health coverage), the additional *negotiated* fee makes it easy for the rich to find a willing donor. The medical director of the New England Organ Bank summarizes the situation as follows:

> What has become evident is that the government is not the source or final arbiter of payments. Market forces ... determine the under the table price – in some instances based upon gender, blood type and age. Thus the Iranian system is (not surprisingly) far from regulated.
>
> (quoted in Griffin 2007: 505)

It is obvious that the Iranian system breaches the principles laid down by WHO and the Declaration of Istanbul concerning transplant commercialism. While it has stopped transplant tourism by its citizens and has apparently prevented international organ trafficking using its donors, it remains a system which discriminates against the poor. Moreover, claims of greater effectiveness and efficiency in dealing with renal disease throughout the whole population seem to be open to question. The conclusion drawn in the *Economist* that we should cease to ban the market in organs seems far from substantiated. So now we can turn to examples where a non-commercial system seems to meet the demand.

Non-market solutions: Spain and Norway

It is well known that rates of organ donation vary widely across the world. For example, a study of changing donation rates in selected countries over the period 1989–99 found a slight increase in the donation rate in the USA (from 16 per million population (pmp) to 21 pmp), a decrease in some European countries (from 16.2 pmp down to 13 pmp in the UK and from 19.7 pmp down to 16.2 in France), but a dramatic rise in Spain (from 14.3 pmp to 33.6 pmp) (Matesanz 2001). Moreover, Spain has continued to maintain this high rate and is consequently reducing its waiting lists for transplants, despite increasing demand. The success of the Spanish programme has led people to speak of 'the Spanish Model' (Matesanz 2003). Another notable feature of this model is that it is almost exclusively sourcing cadaveric organs (99 per cent of renal transplants are cadaveric and only 1 per cent are from living donors). Matesanz explains the success of the scheme in terms of a systematic approach to organ retrieval:

> The organ shortage is not due to a lack of potential donors, but rather a failure to turn many potential into actual donors ... This success [of the Spanish Model] is due to a proactive donor detection programme performed by well trained transplant coordinators, introduction of systematic death audits in hospitals, and the combination of a positive social atmosphere, an adequate management of mass media relations, and on [sic] adequate economic re-imbursement for the hospitals.
>
> (Matesanz 2004: 739)

A quite different example of a successful donor recruitment system comes from Norway. Here there has been a high rate of donation from *related living* donors (39 per cent of all transplantations on 2002 figures) and also a very high transplantation rate (45–47 transplants pmp) (Jakobsen *et al.* 2003). At the same time, the Norwegians have sustained a high cadaveric transplant rate (28.7 pmp). The result is that they have been able to maintain one of the shortest waiting lists in the world (Jakobsen 1996; Rudge 2003), although in common with other countries this has recently shown a considerable increase (Skjøld 2004).

These two national examples illustrate that unpaid systems of organ procurement can work effectively and efficiently. But how has this been achieved? Clearly it must be a combination of legislative, organizational and cultural factors. One legislative factor might be the enactment of 'presumed consent' or 'opt out' laws. Such laws do not require the active consent of the deceased donor (e.g. by carrying a donor card or entering one's name on a register), but presume consent unless the donor has opted out. Both Spain and Norway have this type of law. However, they also allow next of kin to veto the removal of the organ. Healy (2006) has shown that, while countries with presumed consent legislation have higher rates of donation, the refusal to allow a next of kin veto does not improve the rate further. Clearly, then, different factors operate to make a difference. One must be cultural attitudes to donation. The very high rate of living related donation in Norway reveals a culture in which the family (even including grandparents!) rally round when renal failure is diagnosed, making sure that a compatible donor is found. It is perhaps surprising that in Asian cultures, where family duties are so important, there is not a higher rate of living related donation. This could be because families in Asia would prefer that strangers take the risks of nephrectomy. Equally in the case of cadaveric donation, cultural attitudes are likely to have a strong influence, including religious views of the integrity of the dead body and a sense of corporate duty to the sick. But, in addition, as is evident from the Spanish Model, what is needed is the right organization. As Healy points out, we need to focus on 'how procurement agencies systematically create opportunities to give, and work to produce a public understanding of why donation is worthwhile' (Healy 2006: 1019). Thus we have returned to the central issue we identified in the discussion of blood donation. If we want to rely on people's 'freedom to give', then we need to create the social structures that create and enhance that freedom.

Conclusion: which future?

I began this chapter with the analogy of the futures market in the financial sector, and I suggested that people could regard their bodies as containing realizable and disposable assets, rather as they might survey their other possessions in a time of difficulty to decide how best to improve their finances. Given the high demand for transplantable organs, people who are strapped for cash, and, even more, those who are short of even the basic necessities of life, can turn to their bodies as their best hope of rescue if an organ market exists (legally or illegally). Of course, there is international condemnation of such commercialization of the body, but things could change. The American Medical Association has voted to re-examine the issue of payment for organs (Council on Ethical and Judicial Affairs, American Medical Association 2002; Josefson 2002; Taub *et al.* 2003), and there are many voices in the bioethics world describing the current ban as irrational and unfair to the poor, as we have seen above. Thus this is a possible future – the body as one's ultimate real estate.

I have tried to show in this chapter why this is the wrong future to aim for, both from a pragmatic and from a moral perspective. The poor are not rescued from their poverty by such a scheme, nor is there any convincing evidence to show that a trade in organs will solve the organ crisis in an equitable manner. Titmuss's insight that a market in blood is both dangerous and inefficient is now widely recognized as substantially correct, and the risks and injustices of a trade in organs are unmistakable. On the other hand, unpaid donation of both blood and organs has been shown to be a viable method of meeting the demand. What we need is a more sustained attempt to provide the structures worldwide in which the evident human drive to help the other in need can be effectively deployed through genuine and voluntary donation. In this way our bodies become a source of connection with others – be they relatives or strangers – rather than a bastion for no more than mere survival in an unjust world.

Chapter 4

The tissue trove

In the previous chapter, I argued that the norm of altruistic giving espoused by Titmuss should remain the determining principle for blood and organ donation. However, things have moved on dramatically since Titmuss issued his challenge to the commercialization of the body and its parts. As Waldby and Mitchell point out, the emergence of what they describe as 'tissue economies' has had a paradoxical effect on what Titmuss saw as the way to ensure social equity:

> Effectively, his strategy to make the human body a bulwark against the commodification of social life, a strategy now institutionalized in bio-ethical procedure, has simply rendered the body an open source of free biological material for commercial use.
>
> (Waldby and Mitchell 2006: 24)

The demand for human tissue from the medical and scientific community and from the biotechnology and pharmaceutical industries is now massive. Andrews and Nelkin sum up the situation in their study of the US market in human tissue, *Body Bazaar*:

> The business of human bodies is a growing part of the $17 billion bio-technology industry comprising more than thirteen hundred biotechnology firms. Those companies extract, analyze, and transform tissue into products with enormous potential for future economic gain. Their demands for skin, blood, placenta, gametes, biopsied tissue, and sources of genetic material are expanding. The blood we all provide routinely for diagnostic purposes is now useful for the study of biological processes and the genetic basis of disease. Infant foreskin can be used to create new tissue for artificial skin. Umbilical cords are valued as a source of stem cells ... Cell lines derived from the kidneys of deceased babies are used to manufacture a common clot-busting drug ... And human DNA can even be used to run computers, since the four chemicals – represented by the letters CATG – provide more permutations than the binary code.
>
> (Andrews and Nelkin 2001: 2f)

This treasure trove of human materials has spawned a new type of criminal – the bio-pirate. Michael Mastromarino, a former dentist who owned a New Jersey based firm called Biomedical Tissue Services (BTS), was convicted in 2008 in a New York court for conspiring with funeral directors in several states to strip the body parts of corpses awaiting burial or cremation, including arm and leg bones, skin and (possibly) heart valves and veins. The products were then sold on to companies providing materials for dental implants, bone implants, skin grafts and many other medical procedures. It emerged that more than one thousand corpses had been 'harvested' in this way. (Bones were replaced with PVC piping or broomsticks to conceal what had been done from the relatives.) More than 10,000 people received these tissues, some of them from persons infected with AIDS or other infectious diseases. Mastromarino was convicted and sentenced to 18 to 54 years in prison. However, it is clear that he is not the first – and probably not the last – 'bio-pirate'. Andrews and Nelkin report several other earlier cases, including the sale of organs and brain parts from an infant by a morgue assistant, the sale of spines by the director of a medical school anatomy mortuary, and the routine sale of body parts, without the knowledge or consent of families, by mortuaries and crematoria in California (2001: 160).

Clearly such practices are utterly unethical, as well as being probably illegal (although the laws under which people can be convicted are somewhat fuzzy and outmoded in many jurisdictions (Brazier and Cave 2007; Skegg 1974, 1988, 1992)). But even if we discount these macabre fringes of the tissue market, what are we to make of the use of the huge amounts of quite legally obtained human tissue held in numerous medical facilities and tissue banks throughout the world? (Estimates of the total amount are very hard to compute, but a calculation of tissue held only in the USA, published in 1999, suggested a total of at least 307 million specimens, with an ongoing accumulation rate of more than 20 million samples per year (see Weir and Olick 2004: Ch. 2).) Does it matter that tissue donated freely and willingly for the purpose of improving medical research can now become a source of major profit for most parties involved, *except* the original donor? If there was consent (at least of some kind), and if no harm is caused to the original donors, why should we be concerned about it?

Property revisited

This turns out to be a complicated question to answer. From both an ethical and a legal perspective we shall have to return again to the issue of property in the body. To deal fully with the ethical issues, we need to look for new paradigms from the ones traditionally used in discussions of the body as commodity. In particular we need to consider whether (as Waldby and Mitchell argue) the simple distinction between gift and sale offered by Titmuss really applies in this much more complex setting. After considering this background to the debate, I shall look at two examples which illustrate the need for new para-digms – the demand for oocytes (the cells in the ovary from which eggs are formed) for research, created by the emergence of stem-cell technology, and the concept of public trust associated with the rapid move towards large-scale collections of tissue and health data, now commonly described as 'biobanks'.

Property after Moore

The whole issue of property rights in human tissue became crystallized in a 1990 decision of the California Supreme Court in Moore v. Regents of the University of California (1990). I shall discuss the circumstances of this case shortly, but first we need to note two other very important developments in the legal background of biotechnology in the USA: the Chakrabarty deci-sion of the US Supreme Court in 1980, and the Bayh–Dole Act passed by the US Congress, also in 1980.

The Chakrabarty case concerned the issuing of a patent, sought by a microbiologist Dr Ananda Chakrabarty (but to be assigned to the General Electric Company), for a genetically engineered bacterium which was cap-able of breaking down multiple components of crude oil, and so was envi-saged to be of considerable use in dealing with oil spills. Chakrabarty made three types of claim: process claims for the method of producing the bacterium; claims for an inoculum composed of carrier material and the bacterium; and claims to the genetically altered bacterium itself. The claims were first lodged in 1972 and they followed a tortuous legal path. The patent examiner allowed the claims for the process and the carrier medium, but disallowed the third claim, for the bacterium, on the grounds (1) that micro-organisms are products of nature and (2) that as living things they are not patentable subject matter. A series of appeals then followed, culminating in the appeal to the Supreme Court by the Commissioner of Patents and Trademarks against a judgment by the Court of Customs and Appeals that the patent should be granted. The Supreme Court rejected the appeal by a slender majority (five to four), thus affirming the decision of the lower court that a patent could be granted for the bacterium – the court, asserting that 'any-thing under the sun that is made by man' could be patented, concluded: 'the patentee has produced a new bacterium with markedly different character-istics from any found in nature and one having the potential for significant utility. His discovery is not nature's handiwork, but his own; accordingly it is patentable subject matter' (Diamond v. Chakrabarty 1980).

Leon Kass, reflecting on the philosophical implications of this decision, saw the court as a 'teacher of shallowness' (1985: 149). If a living organism is no more than a composition of matter, he asked, what does this assessment mean for the status of other living organisms, including human beings themselves. The court, by discounting the fact that the bacterium was a living being, had failed to see that it was in effect teaching philosophical materialism, in which all that truly *is* is matter. This implies a kind of homogeneity in nature, and so 'the absence of any special dignity in all living nature, our own included (Kass 1985: 150). I shall return to the question of whether it is correct to treat living tissue as the same as any other material – at least when it is derived from human sources – at the end of this chapter, when I suggest the norm of 'respect for our common humanity' as a guide to how we should proceed.

If Chakrabarty provided a *legal justification* for the commercial exploitation of living matter, the Bayh–Dole Act provided the *means* for federally funded university researchers to turn their research efforts to profit for their institutions and also for themselves. The new law allowed universities to retain ownership of inventions made under federally funded research. In return universities were expected to file for patent protection and to ensure commercialization upon licensing. The royalties from such ventures were to be shared with the inventors; a proportion provided to the university and department or college; and the remainder used to support the technology transfer process. The Technology Transfer Office of Colorado State University Research Foundation notes the major outcomes of this Act:

> Prior to Bayh–Dole, fewer than 250 patents were issued to universities per year. In FY 2000, there were over 330 U.S. and Canadian institutions and universities engaged in technology transfer ... University-industry collaborations have helped move new discoveries from the lab to the market place faster and more efficiently than ever before – ensuring that products and services based on federally funded research reach the public ... University gross licensing revenues exceeded $200M in 1992 and by 1992 that number had risen to $250M. In FY 2000, U.S. and Canadian institutions and universities Gross Licensing Income is reported in the AUTM survey at $1.26 Billion.
>
> (Colorado State University Research Foundation 2006)

The combination of Chakrabarty and Bayh–Dole opened wide the door for the commercialization of human tissue and cell lines, provided the licensee had produced something novel through the exercise of skill and labour. Thus we come to the celebrated case of Moore v. Regents of the University of California, which raised in a dramatic form the position of the donor of tissues, when large profits have been made from their commercial exploitation.

In 1976, John Moore was diagnosed with hairy cell leukaemia, a rare and potentially fatal disease. He consulted Dr David Golde at the UCLA Medical Center in Los Angeles and, following his advice, had his spleen surgically removed. The clinical care he received appeared to be entirely appropriate and effective. However, Dr Golde and a research associate had noticed from the very first visit of the patient that there was potential commercial value in

Moore's blood cells, because of their unusual properties. Over the next seven years Moore was asked to travel regularly from his home in Seattle to the UCLA Medical Center to give additional samples of bone, blood, skin, bone marrow aspirate and sperm. He was told that these samples were necessary to ensure his continuing health. In fact, however, Golde and his associates were developing an immortal cell line, which they named 'Mo', after the patient. In the early 1980s they began the process of filing for a patent and were granted it in 1984. Dr Golde and his associate Dr Quan were named as inventors and the California State Regents as the assignees. This turned out to be of huge financial value to both Golde and his university. Entirely in the spirit of Bayh-Dole, Golde and the Regents negotiated a commercial deal with two private companies, which included share options and annual payments to Golde and the university. By 1990, the potential commercial value of the patent was estimated at $3.01 billion.

Moore only discovered what was happening in 1983, when he was asked to sign a consent form, which was very unlike those he had previously signed. The form asked him to grant to the university any and all rights he and his heirs might have in any cell line developed from his blood or bone marrow. He refused to sign, and, on learning about the patent for the 'Mo' cell line, brought a lawsuit against the Regents of the university, the two researchers and the firms with which they had negotiated the financial agreement. This legal process eventually ended up in the Supreme Court of California, with judgment issued in 1990. The Court ruled on two issues: whether Golde's failure to disclose his research project and his financial interests was a breach of his fiduciary duty; and whether Moore was entitled to a share in the profits from the 'Mo' cell line, as compensation for violating his property rights in the tissue. The Court ruled in favour of the first claim, but (by a narrow majority) against the second. (The above summary of the Moore case is based on the excellent description and discussion of it in Weir and Olick 2004, where further detail can be found.)

Although Moore v. The Regents of the University of California was a case in one American state, its international importance is very high. Its effect is to deny (albeit with dissenting views) any claims to ownership over those parts of the body which patients have voluntarily given over to hospitals or medical researchers, *even though* the purpose for which they would be used was not disclosed. Weir and Olick summarize this decision as follows:

> the court seemed implicitly to conclude that the general principle of statutes governing disposal of removed biological materials applies equally to Moore's situation, namely, that any ownership interest in his cells was abandoned when his tissues were removed with his consent. That the consent was not informed does not vitiate this conclusion.
>
> (Weir and Olick 2004: 160)

It is noteworthy that the majority view also saw issues of public policy in the need to deny ownership in the 'abandoned' samples to the donor, for, it was argued, this would have a disastrous effect on a public good, namely, bio-medical research. Although the dissenting opinions raised questions about both the 'abandonment' claim and the public good argument, the majority view seems to remain internationally normative. With a few exceptions,[1] donors of samples or their families cannot expect any financial gain from the contribution of their biological material to research, even though the research may lead to substantial profits for the researchers and their institutions. Indeed, it is now becoming a common practice to state this explicitly on consent forms (for example in the UK Biobank project, which is discussed later in this chapter). But one may reasonably ask whether what seems to be an established *legal* judgment is *ethically* justified. Why should anyone, except the person providing the raw material for the patented invention, be entitled to profit from the use of a person's bodily material? What ethical principles can justify this discrimination?

Beyond Titmuss

To explore the ethical dimensions of this problem, I shall return first to Waldby and Mitchell's argument that, with the advent of a global tissue economy, Titmuss's distinction between gift and sale is too stark and simplistic. These authors identify five new features of the current donation, use and exchange of human tissue: fractionization and fragmentation; globalization; intellectual property in living entities; added value through circulation; and informational interconnectivity. I shall briefly consider each of these in turn, both summarizing and developing further the points made by these authors.

Fractionization and fragmentation

The model in Titmuss's depiction of the gift relationship was of one person donating an object (a quantum of blood or an organ) to another (unknown) person. However, the technology of tissue transfer is now much more complex. Blood is frequently fractionated into a number of components, plasma, red cells, white cells and platelets, some or all of which may be given to one or more recipients, and the recipients themselves may receive blood products from more than one donor. Moreover, other aspects of tissue engineering are even more complex and fragmented, with 'tissue sourced from one person distributed in altered forms along complex pathways to multiple recipients at different times and at different locations throughout the world' (Waldby and Mitchell 2006: 22). This means that we cannot see tissue donation as a simple act of civic responsibility between one citizen and another. Rather there is a complex network of relationships in which the altruistic and the commercial are irrevocably intertwined.

Globalization

It is clear that one specific national institution – the British National Health Service (NHS) – was in Titmuss's mind when he wrote his work. He feared that this great public affirmation of civic responsibility was in real danger of being undermined by the privatization of health care. (This debate continues in the UK to the present time!) But the ideal of such national boundaries to tissue trading is now quite unrealistic with the advent of the global economy. Transnational companies can circumvent national regulatory barriers, sourcing their product in one country and selling it in another. An early example of this was the purchase of Factor VIII by the UK blood service from the USA, where it is legal to pay donors for blood products of this kind. (The disastrous consequences for British haemophiliacs were not foreseen.) Now there is a global market in tissues of all kinds, of which notable examples are ova, sperm and embryonic cell lines.

Intellectual property rights in living organisms

The Chakrabarty decision, as we saw earlier, paved the way for a whole new industry profiting from novel cell lines, new organisms, of which the Harvard onco-mouse is a famous example, and genetic sequences. This is a rapidly expanding global market, attracting venture capital and other forms of financing. The US biotechnology industry increased its revenue from $8 billion in 1992 to $39.2 billion in 2003, and its capital value from $45 billion in 1994 to $311 billion in 2004 (Robinson and Medlock 2005). Given figures like these, the insistence that donors should receive no payment may seem naïve and unjust.

Circulating value

As is evident from the above features of the global tissue market, the rigid distinction between gift and commodity promoted by Titmuss is very hard to maintain. The original gift, through its circulation in a highly complex market, attains an added commercial value with the inevitable interpenetration of public and commercial agencies. There is then no pure realm of gift in this context, which can be insulated from transactions in the market. Waldby and Mitchell sum this up as follows: 'Such rapid transformations of status, in and out of waste, gift, and commodity forms, typify the forms of circulating value assumed by human tissues today' (2006: 26).

Informational interconnectivity

Finally, it is important to note that much of the value of tissue today relates to the information it generates. It has become a platitude to describe our time as the 'information age', but certainly in the realm of biotechnology the economic power of information is a key feature. The value of tissue is often its informational uniqueness (the 'Mo' cell line is a clear example of how particular forms of biological material carry within them highly valuable information). Thus again we are far removed from the simplicity of the life-saving blood donation or organ transplant, in which one individual gives direct benefit to another. Instead tissue yields information that is potentially beneficial to countless individuals, for example those suffering from a specific disease. Another aspect of this informational value arises in the field of pharmacogenomics, where information about a specific ethnic group may help to target effective therapies. The question thus shifts from who owns *the material* to who owns the *information derived from the material* and to what extent this information should be sequestered for private interests, as opposed to being put into the public domain for the benefit of all. In this context we need to look at the altruism of donors, not in relation to personal ownership of, or profit from, the material, but in relation to control of the information derived from the material. (This issue can be spelled out more clearly when we discuss biobanking later in this chapter (pp. 66–71.)

However, if we need to go beyond the simple idea of a gift relationship when considering these complex aspects of the tissue economy, where are we to find our ethical bearings? One possible solution might be a more nuanced understanding of the notion of property in the body. This is a route favoured by several commentators, including Dickenson (2007) and Weir and Olick (2004).

We recall from Chapter 2 that the classical account of property formulated by Honoré sees it as a bundle of rights, rather than a single claim. Could we then disaggregate this bundle when discussing human tissue, removing some of the 'sticks' from the bundle? I already noted in my earlier discussion of these property rights that the contentious ones were those relating to income and capital, since these lead us into the territory of the commodification of body parts. But should these sticks be kept in the bundle when we consider the new types of tissue economies that have emerged? Dickenson (2007) seems ambivalent on this question. On the one hand, she argues that in cases like the 'harvesting' of oocytes for research there is at least a *prima facie* case for asserting that the labour expended by the female donor confers a Lock-ean property right on the donor. On the other hand, she is cautious in taking this to the conclusion that this entitles women to sell their eggs (Dickenson 2007: 70). In the case of Moore, she argues that while rights to income and capital are not appropriate, since he did not expend any labour on the tissue removed – unlike the researchers at UCLA – he should have been granted rights against unauthorized removal and over the subsequent use and management of his tissues.

Like Dickenson, Weir and Olick (2004) oppose the granting of full prop-erty rights to the donors of tissue, to the extent that they can regard them as equivalent to sellable material possessions, but at the same time they reject the notion of 'abandonment', which would give the research institutions *unlimited* property rights in the tissue. Instead they propose that the researchers' property rights are limited in important ways. They wish to protect donors' continued management and use rights of the samples, at least to the extent that a donor may at any time require that any identified or linked samples are withdrawn from research use and destroyed. More contentiously, they propose not only the disclosure to donors of any potential profits from the use of the tissue, but also an undertaking by the researcher to devote a 'reasonable percentage (5%–10%) of any commercial profits from the study ... to one or more identified charitable organizations' (Weir and Olick 2004: 17).

These proposals offer some kind of mediating position between the stark contrast of gift versus sale advocated by Titmuss and criticized by Waldby and Mitchell. I shall now consider what such a position might mean in two different contexts: the provision of oocytes for research and the setting up of major collections of tissues and health information for research purposes – biobanking.

Human eggs for research

The rapid development of stem-cell science has led to an escalating demand for research oocytes in order to facilitate study of so-called 'therapeutic cloning' or somatic cell nuclear transfer (SCNT). The hope is that this research will lead to the development of stem-cell therapies, using histologically compatible cells. Waldby (2008) has surveyed the rapidly developing global market in such reproductive material. There are a number of important aspects of this particular section of the global tissue market: the number of oocytes required; the risks entailed in obtaining them; the overlap between the sourcing of eggs for reproduction and for research; and the phenomenon of global trading.

Quantity of oocytes

Study of the work of the disgraced Korean scientist Hwang Woo Suk reveals how many oocytes are required to produce research results. In one paper he reported using 242 oocytes from 16 donors to produce one cell line (Hwang *et al.* 2004). The enquiry by his own university into his activities revealed that over a three-year period he used 2061 oocytes from a total of 129 women (Steinbrook 2006). There are, of course, other issues relating to Hwang's activities, notably the veracity of his research claims and his inappropriate use of his own research assistants as donors, but no one has suggested that the quantity of oocytes used was unusual for this type of research. When we consider how many countries are now promoting stem-cell research, the scale of the demand becomes evident.

Risks

Moreover, the method of obtaining the oocytes is much more invasive and associated with risk than (for example) obtaining blood or sperm. Dickenson (2007: 63) states that it is arguably more risky than the excision of a kidney, since it entails stopping the normal reproductive process, hyperstimulating the ovaries and then surgically removing the oocytes under anaesthesia. Steinbrook (2006: 324) gives details of the process, which includes up to 56 hours in a medical setting, daily injections for seven to ten days and discomfort and possible bleeding from the retrieval procedure. In addition, women may develop ovarian hyperstimulation syndrome (OHSS), which involves pain, abdominal inflammation, possible renal failure and infertility, venous thrombo-embolism and cardiac instability (Waldby 2008). While the risk of severe OHSS may be quite rare, and its more severe forms more likely when egg retrieval is followed by pregnancy (Sauer 2001), it is clearly the case that the procedure cannot be described as risk free.

Association with reproduction

The association between the sourcing of oocytes for in vitro fertilization (IVF) to help the infertile and the sourcing for research use is another significant feature of the rapidly expanding global market. In the UK the Human Fertilization and Embryology Authority (HFEA) has sought to increase the supply of oocytes for research by allowing payment of up to £250 as well as discounted IVF services for women willing to donate (HFEA 2007). This is perhaps surprising in a country which is officially opposed to a market in gametes. However, there are plenty of countries where the selling of gametes is entirely legal, notably the USA, in which there is a thriving market in 'premium' gametes – sperm from Nobel Prize winners, for example, and ova from good-looking Caucasian Ivy League undergrads. Waldby (2008: 25) quotes figures from the US Centers for Disease Control and Prevention, showing that over 13,000 reproductive procedures performed in the USA in 2002 used purchased oocytes.

Global trading

It is hardly surprising, then, that a global market in research oocytes seems to be developing as an extension to the already strong market in oocytes for reproduction. In the USA there are no federal regulations or laws which could prevent such an extension. Moreover, since the individual characteristics of the donor are irrelevant when it comes to stem-cell research, there is a much larger pool of potential sellers. As Waldby observes:

In the U.S., the juxtaposition of poor, ghettoized populations with high technology corridors – for example, around Boston, Bethesda, Raleigh-Durham and Southern California – makes these kinds of markets even more feasible. Here we can see an internal version of the extraterritorial trade ... with poor female populations within the nation-state acting as potential vendors for national biotechnology industries.

(Waldby 2008: 26)

So far as the international scene is concerned, Waldby points to the well-documented spread of 'reproductive tourism', through which national prohibitions on gamete sales are circumvented by setting up clinics in less regulated countries, such as Spain, Crete and former Soviet bloc countries. In Asia there was a similar arrangement between Korea and Japan, with a brokerage company called DNA-BANK enabling Japanese couples to purchase reproductive oocytes from Korean sources, and here the link with research oocytes becomes totally clear, since Hwang used the same firm to obtain his research material. Waldby envisages a similar situation developing in China and India, since they have 'large impoverished populations, extensive networks of fertility clinics ... and burgeoning stem cell industries, setting the scene for exploitative forms of oocyte procurement' (2008: 27). She concludes that, although the women supplying this material are usually classed as 'donors' and their contribution is – in official statements at least – described as a gift, with perhaps some compensation, the reality is that they are vendors, and poorly protected ones at that. Their contribution is best thought of 'as reproductive labour in the lower circuits of the reproductively based biotechnology industries' (Waldby 2008: 27). As we saw earlier, Dickenson reaches a very similar conclusion. Discussing how 'the lady vanishes' in discussion of stem-cell research, she argues that 'women labour to produce extracted ova, in the purposeful manner characterising the sort of labour which grounds property rights in Locke' (Dickenson 2007: 68).

What practical steps would follow from such a recognition of women's reproductive labour in stem-cell research? Here Waldby and Dickenson differ. For Dickenson a move to the whole range of property rights in the oocytes including the rights to income and capital would be ill advised, because it would encourage 'the untrammeled commodification of practically everything' (2007: 69). Instead, she proposes a contractual arrangement between the women donating and the users of their oocytes that would safeguard two of the property rights in the bundle – protection against unauthorized taking (through proper consent procedures) and the right to determine the management of one's tissue's use. The assertion of this second right indicates a rejection of the 'abandonment' concept, by asserting the woman's continued interest in the tissue after it has been taken from her body. Waldby, on the other hand, steps boldly into the territory of employment law, acknowledging that in doing so she is contravening the European ethos of opposition to commodifying the human body. She argues that the more abusive aspects of the global trade in women's reproductive tissue merit intervention by international human rights agencies similar to those used to deal with the abuses of the global sex trade. But, in addition, she argues that we need an approach to oocyte supply 'that combines issues of safety, consent and clinical conditions with those of workers' rights, organized representation for vendors and negotiation of conditions' (Waldby 2008: 29).

Here, then, are two possible approaches to the reality of the current rapid expansion in international trade in human tissue. In the last section of this chapter (pp. 71–3), I shall discuss the adequacy of these and other proposed solutions, but, first, we shall explore the issues raised by a different use of tissue, its storage and use for a wide range of health research in repositories described as 'biobanks'.

Biobanks, altruism and trust

The term 'biobank' has come into common use, despite considerable lack of clarity about its exact meaning. It usually denotes a very large collection of biological samples or genetic data which can be linked to the lifestyle and health history of those individuals from whom the samples were obtained. Thus biobanks provide a rich resource for research projects of all sorts that seek to establish connections between genetic or biological, epidemiological and lifestyle factors leading to disease. They may also be used to estimate the effectiveness of current therapeutic interventions, and could provide the data needed to target therapies at specific groups (pharmacogenetics). Beyond these similarities, however, biobanks vary greatly. Some are retrospective (linking already collected samples and other data); others are prospective, recruiting volunteers who are willing to provide samples and other information and to have their health records interrogated over decades. Some entail linkages between different databases and tissue banks, without obtaining the consent of the individuals whose data are stored and using mechanisms like coding and 'trusted third parties' to safeguard the identity of the individuals; others (normally the prospective projects) obtain individual consent for access to the samples and data, but (since the details of the research cannot be known in advance) have to rely on very 'open' or 'broad' consent.

It is obvious that biobanks raise a whole range of ethical issues, such as the validity of broad consent, the risks to participants (mainly in terms of breaches of privacy), the security of the data storage and of the access mechanisms, the potential for unauthorized or damaging access to the resource (for example by employers or insurance companies), and the appropriate uses of the resource as a whole by researchers and commercial enterprises. (I have surveyed these issues in Campbell 2007.) For the purposes of this chapter, however, I shall focus on just one example – the UK Biobank – and on one of the ethical topics – how the altruism and trust exhibited by participants in the bank is to be honoured and safeguarded.

The UK Biobank aims to recruit 500,000 volunteers over a period of about four years, drawn from the UK population of persons aged between 40 and 69. Potential participants are identified from centrally held health registration records (virtually all people in the UK are registered with a general practitioner) and sent a letter of invitation to attend an assessment centre. A pamphlet gives them basic information about the project and if they visit the assessment centre they are able to consent or withdraw from the study after receiving fuller information. Those who participate fill in a very detailed questionnaire, have a set of basic measurements taken (such as blood pressure and body mass index), give samples of blood and urine, and agree to access to their health records (with safeguards for confidentiality) for subsequent years (unless they later withdraw from the study). In signing the consent form they agree to all these terms and in addition agree that, although there may be commercial gain from the use of their samples and data, they will not receive any form of payment at any stage. They are also informed that participation is not a 'health check' and that apart from some basic data from the assessment visit, they will not receive any individual results from the subsequent work on their data and samples. Their reason for agreeing, then, must be because they want to share in the mission of the project, which is (as stated in its tag line) 'improving the health of future generations'. (For full details of the project, see UK Biobank (2007).)

It is important to recognize the high degree of commitment of those who respond positively to requests to enrol in projects of this nature. As we have seen, not only do the participants in UK Biobank agree to the taking of a set of physical measurements and the donation of samples and to answering what could be seen as an intrusive questionnaire about their health and life-style, they also grant full access to their health records, past and future, up to and beyond their death, unless they withdraw from the project. Such a major and long-term commitment must depend on both a strong motivation to assist in the project and a high level of trust in the organization carrying it out. How, then, can one ensure that such altruism and trust are safeguarded and accorded the respect that is due? The following three measures seem to be essential components that must be incorporated into any governance regime for biobanks: (1) genuine participation and partnership; (2) independent scrutiny; and (3) public openness and accountability.

Participation and partnership

The research community is slowly beginning to change the language of involvement in biomedical research by patients and the general public. Research 'subjects' have become research 'participants', and some genuine attempts have been made to involve consumer groups in determining relevant research projects. For biobanks – especially those dependent on volunteers from the community at large – such a change, not only of language but also of attitude, is vital. The project will be a true success only when a majority of those enrolled become active and interested participants in the evolving resource, especially when it begins to attract applications and proposals from researchers who wish to use the material stored by the resource for specific projects.

It is important to note the ethical dimension of such endeavours. Ensuring genuine participation and partnership is not part of the project of protecting individual rights. Rather, it supports and reinforces the altruism that motivated the participants in the first place. This means that proposals to give participants a say in the uses of their samples (see Kaye *et al.* 2004; and Dickenson's idea of management rights over donated oocytes, described on pp. 65–6) may fail to meet this need for partnership. Indeed, they could be seen as undercutting it. Normally, donation carries with it a willing surrender of individual control of the donated material. For example, donors of blood or kidneys have no right to determine the recipients of their donation. The requirement, then, is not to try to create some form of participant control. This would, in any case, be contrary to the stated aim of such projects, which is to enhance the health of all, not just of participants. However, participants' awareness of how the project is developing, and their input into how best it might meet its aims, would be invaluable. Partnership of this kind requires sophisticated and effective ongoing communication with participants at very regular intervals. The key governance challenges here lie in crafting effective practical measures to enable genuine, meaningful participation and partnership to be established.

Yet, can we speak genuinely of partnership if the donors have no say at all in how the resource is managed in the future? Is this any more than token consultation, with the only power available to donors being a quite passive and negative one – the right to withdraw, wholly or in part, from the project as a whole? (The current policy for withdrawal allows for three levels: no further contact; no further use of the samples or interrogation of the health records; and withdrawal of the samples and their destruction.) Winickoff (2007) has argued for a stronger role for donors in the subsequent policy decisions of the biobank on matters such as access, priority of use and matters of intellectual property. Commenting on the claims made in the UK Parliament that UK Biobank Ltd would represent a partnership between this research endeavour and the public, Winickoff remarks:

> Parliamentary rhetoric aside, donors possess little control share, and no equity share, in the common pool resource. The donors do enjoy the right to withdraw as individual donors, and a vague sort of representation by the Ethics and Governance Council. Thus, though donors may be "partners" in a limited sense, they have no role in institutional governance. By failing to provide for some governance role for the donors,

project planners have lost an important potential strength: from the perspective of pragmatism, some mechanism of meaningful representation of the donor collective could greatly enhance both participation rate, participant trust, and by extension, project sustainability.

(Winickoff 2007: 446)

As a mechanism to remedy this weakness, Winickoff proposes the setting up of a Donors' Association, which could elect its own officers and could obtain representation on both the Board of Directors of UK Biobank and of the Ethics and Governance Council. Justifying this move, Winickoff points out that the donors are in a sense contributors of both capital (the samples and health information) and, in some cases, labour (those donors who agree to further contact). We could say, then, that they are shareholders and should be represented. The idea is a stimulating one and it certainly raises in an appropriate way the real risk that claims to partnership are mere rhetoric. Yet the difficulty in the concept (as I alluded to already earlier) is that it seems to give the donor group an inappropriate say in how the resource is used. Clearly they should be consulted and membership on the Ethics and Governance Council seems very appropriate. But it is not so clear that donors have a right to help to decide on priorities of access and use. Such decisions will be very complex ones, and there is no reason to suppose that a person participating in such a massive project would have *ipso facto* a special understanding of the issues involved. For this reason, representation on executive bodies may not be the way to go. Nevertheless, the question of who is to be trusted to ensure that the public good is served, especially when there will be strong commercial interests wanting to use the resource, remains a crucial one. As I suggest below, independent oversight may be a better way to ensure that the public trust is honoured.

Independent oversight

Most large-scale biobank projects have some kind of ethics oversight body, though this may not necessarily deal only with that project. UK Biobank appears to have the most extensive arrangements of this kind in the world. Its own protocol, and all research proposals that it considers, must be approved by an NHS research ethics committee. In addition UK Biobank is bound to act in accordance with an Ethics and Governance Framework (EGF), and it is monitored by an independent Ethics and Governance Council (EGC) appointed by the funders of the project. An important aspect of the monitoring undertaken by the EGC is that it has full access to all activities of UK Biobank and it reports its findings regularly to the public. Since public confidence and trust are essential to the success of any large-scale biobanking project, this public reporting element constitutes a potentially powerful oversight device. Any such monitoring body has to be fully involved in decisions about granting access to the resource, since these entail ethical as well as scientific questions. Biobanks that enlist people on the promise that a resource will be used to improve the health of future generations cannot escape the difficult task of deciding where the priorities in health research should lie in order to give preference to those researchers whose projects appear most likely to bring about genuine improvements in public health. Thus, independent monitoring bodies have a major role to play in helping to establish criteria for prioritizing access – especially to the depletable parts of the resource – and in ensuring their implementation.

Openness and accountability

Finally, as noted above, regular reports by an independent oversight body can help to ensure that biobanks remain accountable to the public whose data and samples they hold. But population biobanks are such massive enterprises that questions of accountability go well beyond the issues that may be debated by an oversight body. In part, this is due to the potentially enormous scope of health applications to which the banked resources may be put, as genetic factors become ever better understood and as the interplay of genetics with lifestyle and environmental factors becomes mapped with ever greater precision and detail. But, in addition, the revolution in electronic data handling, amalgamation, long-term storage, networking, interlinking and searchability holds huge potential for both benign and less than benign applications. Conceivably, genetic databases originally set up exclusively for biomedical research and public health purposes could become exploited for other ends, or be linked up with multiple other datasets. Accordingly, the existence and potential of a large-scale biobank cannot be treated in isolation from broader questions relating to the delicate balance between personal privacy and public good.

Particularly relevant here is the fact that in Europe, while national biobanks and population biobanks are being developed relatively slowly, there are rapid expansions in forensic DNA databases. The UK is a prime example. Since its inception in 1995, the police National DNA Database has burgeoned into the largest criminal intelligence database of its kind in the world. Currently, it holds over 3.5 million samples. On average, some 40,000 new individual DNA profiles are added to it each month by the police in England and Wales (Nuffield Council on Bioethics 2007). Much of its exponential growth has been due to what has been, to date, increasingly permissive legislation authorizing DNA sample retention by the police. This highlights the fact that forensic DNA databases are subject to quite different laws and criteria governing their control and use from other collections, such as those established and used for biomedical research. Even so, there are good reasons to suggest that forensic collections, too, ought to be managed and scrutinized with equivalent levels of openness, independent ethical oversight and public accountability (Human Genetics Commission 2002).

For these reasons, large-scale population biobanks – of whatever description – must not be allowed to develop without full public debate and accountability to the public at large. There is no question that the motivations of all parties – from the funders, through the scientists involved, to those who volunteer their data and samples – are entirely beneficent. But ensuring constant public accountability and full public scrutiny is essential lest such altruism become translated into social solidarity, and social solidarity in turn become the imposition of measures for the general 'public good', including national security. Such concerns – and especially the fear that biomedical biobanks could be commandeered and exploited by a future governing regime for other uses, which supposedly serve the 'public good' but sacrifice individual rights and interests – may prove to be unjustified. But it will be worth ensuring that the safeguards are in place to prevent a future generation or malign political regime turning these rich databases into instruments for social control or private profit. Instead, we have to ensure that they are genuinely a shared resource, devoted to the common good of the society from which the altruistic donors were recruited. It is to this concept of a shared and open resource in human tissue that I finally turn.

A common humanity

Throughout this chapter, I have been seeking conceptualizations of the 'tissue trove' that safeguard its human origin and its basis in altruism, without naïvely imagining that we can exclude all commercial elements from the exploitation of this vast resource. How can we hold on to the idea of the common good of humanity, when the forces of commercial gain are so powerful in this area of research and development? Kissell (2000) has offered the term 'human non-subject research' (HNR) as a way of conceptualizing the issues without confusing them with the traditional questions of consent and harm/benefit raised by human subject research:

> HNR encompasses any experimentation or procedure that deals with human material that is separated from the donor's body – nucleic acid, genetic sequences, genes, cells, blood, organs and so forth – and that does not, therefore, affect the personal-physiological functioning of its donor-source[2] ... The materials are human in origin, but they have only an ambiguous relationship to persons.
>
> (Kissell 2000: 178)

Kissell goes on to discuss how the human material covered by HNR is best categorized. She rejects as 'short-sighted' what she sees as two extremes: an essentialist view that seeks some special definition of 'human' that will set the material off from other objects in a category of its own; and a property approach, which falsely disjoins the material from the person from whom it is taken, failing to see both its uniqueness and its connection through genetic linkage to humanity as a whole. In place of these simplifications she wants us to consider how the use of materials from our own and others' bodies shows humankind to be the 'self-determining creator of its own meaning, in light of the potential provided by advances in biotechnology' (Kissell 2000: 178). For Kissell, then, the use of bodily material puts a special responsibility on to us, as creators or destroyers of our own destiny.

Such language may seem somewhat high-flown to those simply seeking an ethical and practical solution to the escalating use of human tissue. Yet it does point to a way of conceptualizing our concern that the tissue market is becoming just another commodities market, on an analogy with a market in oil, or corn or gold. Another way of putting this is to say that human heritage issues are evoked by the prospect of the human body as some kind of goldmine. (Dickenson translates a memorable statement by the French writer Baud: 'Which is more damaging for the human person: to consider his body and everything belonging to it as things rigorously protected by property law, or to admit that anything detached from the body has the same status as excrement, but excrement that can be turned to gold' (quoted in Dickenson 2007: 158).) We are, one might say, haunted by the feeling that the global tissue market is not just potentially exploitative; it is in some sense damaging our common humanity.

Perhaps, then, the solution is to move from a focus on individual owner-ship to a broader concept of a community resource – provided, of course, the individual is protected from unauthorized taking of her tissue and from exploitative market practices. If this is the right direction to move in, then Dickenson's idea of giving individual donors continuing control over the use of their tissue (for example Moore's cell line or a donated oocyte used in stem-cell work) seems the wrong solution. But equally, Waldby's approach in terms of workers' rights and protections seems a surrender to the idea that the tissue market is no more than another instance of the need to regulate vendor–purchaser relationships, in other words a market like any other.

What might be the alternative, one that sees a special responsibility in the collection and use of human tissue? One of the dissenting Justices in the *Moore* case, Broussard J, made some interesting remarks on this topic:

> It is certainly arguable that as a matter of policy or morality it would be wiser to prohibit any private individual or entity from profiting from the fortuitous value that adheres in a part of the human body and instead to require all valuable excised body parts to be deposited in a public repo-sitory which would make such materials freely available to all scientists for the betterment of society as a whole.
>
> (quoted in Dickenson, 2007: 15)

The metaphor of a commons which must be protected from enclosure by commercial interests seems to point a way forward: and it is one extensively discussed in the literature and used by both Dickenson (2007: Ch. 8) and by Waldby and Mitchell (2006: Ch. 5). In this conceptualization human materials and the information derived from them should be openly accessible so that they can be used for the benefit of all humankind, rather than for the profit of the powerful. It is clear from our discussion of biobanking that this is a major ethical concern for altruistic donors of tissue for research. Such people seek to leave a legacy of better health for future generations and are willing to share both their bodily materials and their health information to support such a cause. Waldby and Mitchell cite the UK Stem Cell Bank as a good example of how public interests can be protected and promoted in an era of mixed private and public enterprise. All stem-cell lines have to be lodged in the bank, which will help maximize access to a range of lines to all researchers, keep costs down and minimize duplication of effort and wastage of resources. At the same time patents will be permitted (but not negotiated by the bank) and commercial enterprises will have access as well as publicly funded researchers. Waldby and Mitchell conclude:

> As a public institution, the bank will help to locate the stem cell research effort in public, national space, even when commercial firms carry it out … While the bank cannot fundamentally alter the structural inequity built into the giving of tissues to increasingly commercialized research bodies, it may ameliorate and dissipate some of its worse effects.
> (Waldby and Mitchell 2006: 82)

So we have here, perhaps not a solution, but at least a direction. Other ways of sharing benefit, such as the allocation of a percentage of profits to charities, suggested by Weir and Olick, or the setting up of partnerships between researchers into specific diseases and the families providing tissue and data, all point in this same direction. The somewhat vague notion of respect for the human body can find an effective grounding in the institutions we create to manage its use. Even in the midst of the ambiguity and complexity of the global tissue economy, we can hopefully insist on our bodily tissues being used in a respectful and effective way, to protect and enhance our common humanity, to safeguard the biocommons.

Chapter 5

The branded body

The English word 'branded' has an interesting ambiguity. On the one hand, it can imply humiliation, mutilation, stigmatization – as in the branded slave, a life of enforced servitude burned into the flesh. On the other hand, in contemporary usage, 'brand' has become synonymous with fashion and its associated social esteem. Those who wear the latest brands in clothes or accessories signal to others that they are totally 'with it' – up to date, attractive, successful and self-confident. In this chapter I shall explore both of these realms of meaning. First, we consider perception of the body as alien and stigmatizing. This has many forms, some originating from the person's self-perception, such as the desire to have limbs amputated (now usually referred to as body image identity disorder – BIID), the desire to change one's biological gender (transsexualism) and the crippling hatred of the body's weight found in anorexia and bulimia; others arise from societal rejection, illustrated in attitudes to the disabled as alien and disturbing. Second, we shall look at the idea of the body as a fashion accessory, illustrated by the meteoric rise of cosmetic (or 'aesthetic') surgery, which caters to people's need to have an enhanced bodily appearance as a passport to social acceptance and success. I shall argue that both of these aspects of the 'branded' body provide graphic illustration of what Leder (1990) called the *dys*appearance of the body – the body as a source of discontent, pain and fear. In conclusion, I shall consider how the concept of respect for our embodied selves could result in a greater harmony between our conscious and aspiring selves and our bodies.

The alien body

In *The Man Who Mistook His Wife for a Hat* (1985), Oliver Sacks gives a poignant and amusing description of what has come to be classified as BIID (First 2004). It concerns a patient who woke up in a hospital bed to discover that there was 'someone's leg' in bed with him, a severed human leg. As it was New Year's Eve, he eventually decided that this was a silly prank by the nurses, who had put a dead person's leg from the dissecting room into his bed. So he grabbed it and threw it out, but inexplicably he fell out after it!

> 'Look at it!' he cried, with revulsion on his face. 'Have you ever seen such a creepy, horrible thing? I thought a cadaver was just dead. But this is uncanny! And somehow – it's ghastly – it seems stuck to me!' He seized it with both hands, with extraordinary violence, and tried to tear it off his body and, failing, punched it in an access [*sic*] of rage.
>
> (Sacks 1985: 54)

As this quotation illustrates, some people come to regard parts of their body as alien, not truly part of their own body. One could describe it as the opposite of the phantom limb experience of amputees, in which the lost limb is still felt to be present. For sufferers from BIID, the affected body part simply should not be there and needs to be removed as soon as possible. Some people take matters into their own hands and attempt amputation themselves. The condition creates a dilemma for the medical profession. Should they collude with the patient's belief and amputate what is clearly (to all but the patient) a normal, healthy body part? In 2000 a major controversy erupted when it emerged that a Scottish surgeon had amputated the healthy limbs of two patients and proposed to do the same to a third (see Dyer 2000). The Scottish surgeon was prevented by his hospital from continuing this practice, and the ethical and legal aspects have been extensively discussed, with some commentators supporting it (Bayne and Levy 2005) and others opposing it (Johnston and Elliott 2002). However, from the perspective of our exploration of embodiment, the relevant issue is not the ethical and moral obligations of the medical profession, but the evidence that persons making this request are not suffering from psychosis or other psychiatric conditions which create delusional thinking (First 2004). They simply do not feel truly themselves until the offending part is removed. It is estimated that several thousand people worldwide may suffer from this disorder (S. Mueller 2007). Opinion differs as to its causes: some have seen it as a form of sexual fetishism (apotemnophilia, erotic attraction to amputees and thinking of oneself as being one – see Money *et al.* 1977); others (First 2004) have related it to gender identity disorder (discussed on pp. 77–8). Sacks's patient was discovered to have a tumour above his parietal lobe, the area of the brain that maps the body image. This has led to the suggestion of a neurological cause for the perception of the limb as alien (Ramachandran and McGeoch 2007).

Whatever the original cause, we are seeing here an extreme example of a disjunction between a person's perception of their body and their understanding of the nature and boundaries of their personal identity – a breakdown in embodiment, which to the person experiencing it cannot be fairly described as some sort of perversion or disorder. One of the research subjects in a recent study of the condition expressed this as follows: 'I am afraid to do this – because I'm afraid if I'm "cured" … it will take away from part of my identity' (L. Mueller 2007).

Trapped in the wrong body

Another graphic example of this breakdown between self-image and the body is the condition described as transsexualism. For the transsexual, the body they were born with, though anatomically and chromosomally of one sex, is incongruent with the gender to which they feel they belong. They feel trapped in the body of the wrong sex. The suffering this causes is sensitively described by the travel writer Jan Morris in her account of her conviction, since the age of three or four, that she should really be a girl:

> I think of it not just as a sexual enigma, but as a quest for unity. For me every aspect of my life is relevant to that quest – not only the sexual impulses, but all the sights, sounds and smells of memory, the influences of buildings, landscapes, comradeships, the power of love and sorrow, the satisfactions of the senses as of the body. In my mind it is a subject far wider than sex … I see it above all as a dilemma neither of the body nor of the brain, but of the spirit.
>
> (Morris 2002: 9)

In Jan Morris's case, what was desired and achieved through hormones and (eventually) surgery was a male-to-female (MF) gender reassignment – and this is simpler surgically and more common than female-to-male (FM). Raymond (1979) reports that there are four to eight times more MF transsexuals than FM ones.

Transsexualism has been included in the international classification of psychiatric disorders since 1980 (*Diagnostic and Statistical Manual of Mental Disorders*, 4th edition (DSM IV) (1996) 302.85), and now both hormone treatment and gender reassignment surgery are accepted medical practice for effecting the desired change. Nevertheless, the definition of the condition and the medical and surgical remedies are not without controversy. (For a good summary of the debate, see Draper and Evans 2006). But, as with the previous topic, the main focus of my analysis is not on the debate about how the medical profession should act, but on the implications of the condition for the concepts of embodiment and personal identity.

Perhaps there is no more graphic illustration of 'why the body matters' than the overwhelming need of transsexuals to change all the physical attributes associated with their anatomical sex. Such people want to feel within themselves, *and* appear to others, as genuinely of the desired gender. They feel only truly themselves when this change is fully successful. In this respect, they are quite different from transvestites, who play the part of the opposite sex, either for commercial gain or for sexual enjoyment, but seem to remain content with their anatomical sexual characteristics. Equally, transsexuals should not be confused with homosexuals, who may wish to assume gender roles and appearances normally associated with the opposite sex. Transsexuals may seek sexual relationships with the opposite sex to their new identity, or they may seek homosexual relationships in terms of their new identity. The key issue for them is not concerned with physical sexual encounters, but whether their reconstructed body feels genuinely part of their own personhood, as opposed to the alien captivity of the previous 'wrong' body. Morris powerfully expresses this need for a sense of wholeness and completion:

> To me gender is not physical at all, but is altogether insubstantial. It is soul, perhaps, it is talent, it is taste, it is environment, it is how one feels, it is light and shade, it is inner music, it is a spring in one's step or an exchange of glances ... It is the essentialness of oneself, the psyche, the fragment of unity.
>
> (Morris 2002: 25)

Of course, we should note that it is now widely accepted that gender is at least partly a social construct, and that the gender roles assigned in different societies and different historical epochs have little or no grounding in the distinguishing physical sexual characteristics of men and women (Wittig 1992 [1981]; hooks 1982; Riley 1988; Butler 1990). But the observation that gender is a social construct does not relate directly to the dilemma of the transsexual. For Jan Morris, for example, the change did mean an inner change to a more 'feminine' way of feeling and acting:

> The more I was treated as a woman the more woman I became ... If I was assumed to be incompetent at reversing cars, or opening bottles, oddly incompetent I found myself becoming. If a case was thought too heavy for me, inexplicably I found it so myself ... I began to find women's conversation in general more congenial.
>
> (Morris 2002: 149)

This can be seen as conforming to a somewhat stereotypical model of femininity (see Draper and Evans 2006: 103), which may indeed be socially constructed. Both MF and FM transsexuals must face complex negotiations in the social integration phase following surgical transformation (Michel et al. 2001). The point is not conformity or otherwise to social norms, but a sense of inner peace and satisfaction with one's own body never felt until its physical characteristics are changed. The experience of the transsexual illustrates very clearly why Cartesian restrictions of personal identity to rationality or Lockean equations of personal identity with disembodied consciousness simply fail to allow for the fundamental human experience of the embodied self.

We turn now to more tragic examples of alienation from the body, in which the rejection of one's corporeality can be literally fatal.

The body despised

For people suffering from the eating disorders of anorexia and bulimia, it is the shape of their body which causes them distress to a point where any perception of fatness is despised. Anorexia is not loss of appetite, as the Greek root implies, but 'a disorder characterized by deliberate weight loss, induced and sustained by the patient' (WHO International Classification of Diseases (ICD) 10, F. 50.0). Bulimia is 'characterized by repeated bouts of overeating and an excessive preoccupation with control of body weight, leading to a pattern of overeating followed by vomiting or use of purgatives' (ICD 10, F50.2).[1] These brief descriptions fail to capture the full range of suffering which people with such eating disorders inflict upon themselves. The range of what the diagnostic manuals describe as 'compensatory behaviour' includes the excessive use of laxatives, of purgatives or diuretics, and (in the case of people with anorexia) punishing exercise regimens. The medical consequences of both conditions can be very serious, and in the case of anorexia fatal.

The common feature of both conditions is a dread of fatness or a morbid fear of weight gain. They occur almost exclusively in Western or other developed societies and are both much more common in women than in men (who constitute about 8 per cent of the anorexic group and 15 per cent of the bulimic group). The age of onset is 15–19 for women, but possibly slightly later for men. In both conditions the sufferers seek to conceal their activities, deny their evident weight loss and can be very resistant to attempts at therapy.

It is obvious that young people suffering from eating disorders present major dilemmas both to their families and to those seeking to offer professional help. At its most dramatic, this presents itself as the question of whether to force-feed someone dying from starvation as a result of their self-induced condition, and, more generally, how much control to try to exercise over the self-destructive behaviour. This tension between paternalism and respect for autonomy has been well explored in the literature (see Draper 2000, 2003; Giordano 2003). However, as before in this chapter, my focus is not on the ethical dilemmas (crucial though these are), but on the significance of these conditions for our understanding of embodiment. Here the comprehensive and illuminating study of the philosophical as well as ethical and social aspects of eating disorders by Simona Giordano (2005) provides the relevant conceptualizations.

Giordano surveys the various medical, scientific and sociological attempts to account for the compulsion sufferers feel to control their body weight and concludes that no single explanation can provide a satisfactory answer: an organic cause cannot be conclusively demonstrated, nor can psychological accounts of family dynamics or sociological accounts of the obsession with thinness encouraged by the media and the fashion industry. All these, she suggests, may have some bearing on understanding both causes and possibly effective interventions, but no single one seems to account for the complexity of the phenomenon. Moreover, what is missing is an understanding of what the fear of fatness *means* to the sufferers in a *moral sense*. Eating disorders are an extreme way of expressing and embodying moral beliefs about the 'goodness' of lightness and the 'badness' of being fat:

> Aesthetic judgments relating to people's shape are in fact judgments relating to people's worth. The fat body is not only *ugly* – and is not *ugly* 'by chance': the fat body symbolizes laziness, indulgence, lack of will power, lack of self-control, and self-disrespect.
>
> (Giordano 2005: 105, italics in original)

Since people with eating disorders are known to be people who place a very high value on control while at the same time lacking self-worth (see Duker and Slade 2002), they are easily seduced by an ethic of perfectionism, driven by shame and guilt in relation to their body's shape and body's needs. Giordano expresses this graphically:

> The body is a chaotic entity, whose needs and passions may fall out of control: many people including anorexics, believe that there is something *moral* in the capacity to control this chaotic body, and something *immoral* in the incapacity to control it.
>
> (Giordano 2005: 131, italics in original)

Thus the despised body of the anorexic or bulimic person is a tragic outcome of a moral tradition which has sought to denigrate the body and elevate the soul or spirit as the 'true self'. We see here a recurrent theme, discussed in an earlier chapter in terms of Leder's account of the body's *dys*appearance. It is obvious that we cannot in fact live without our body, nor can we find fulfilment, if we experience our bodily needs and bodily appearance as a constant embarrassment – the badly behaved child that we constantly want to hide from public view. Yet, for some people, what Giordano calls 'the value of lightness' has so taken them over that the body, which is in fact part of who they are, becomes merely an endless source of self-disgust and self-punishment. Gordon graphically describes one view of the painful loneliness which this creates:

> One patient offered a dramatic statement about her existential aloneness, comparing her feeling of herself with the Statue of Liberty, the 'lady of the harbor … like the statue, untouched and untouchable, on a little island on the gray ocean, with no relationship to anybody and anything.
>
> (Gordon 1990: 68)

The rejected body

Up to this point we have been considering the 'alien body' primarily as it is viewed from within the person, though clearly external images of the 'good body' have a part to play, especially in the case of eating disorders. Now we turn to the rejection of the body by society, some of which may be mirrored by the rejected person herself. There is a long history of contemptuous or prurient attitudes to 'freaks', with their evident difference used as a form of entertainment for the crowds. Famous examples from the nineteenth century – the 'golden age' of the freak show – are Joseph Merrick, the Elephant Man, and Chang and Eng, the original 'Siamese Twins', who made a good living for themselves as performers. Notwithstanding the persistence of an interest in 'otherness', we live in an apparently more enlightened age now, with an emphasis on the rights of the disabled, stemming from the UN distinctions between impairment, disability and handicap (see UN 1983). These distinctions make it clear that a person is *handicapped* by a combination of physical or psychological abnormality or loss (*impairment*), the consequent restriction on the normal range of human activity (*disability*) and the limiting effects of the environment in which they try to perform the activities. Obvious examples of environmentally created handicaps are the lack of wheelchair access in public buildings or public transport and the lack of non-visual clues for the edges of pavements or the floors of elevators. The distinctions have been largely supported by disability rights activists, since they provide a focus for legislation to remove environmental impediments. At the same time, they can be seen as too simplistic, by suggesting that it is obvious what a 'normal range' of human activity is, whereas there is in fact a huge variation in human ability (see Wendell 1996: 14ff.). Another problem is that 'impairment' may itself be socially constructed. For example, the deaf community has argued strongly in recent times that they should not be seen as being 'impaired', but rather as being 'differently abled'. This has led to the (contentious) decision of some deaf couples to deliberately produce a deaf child.

Another whole dimension of disability rights relates not to the disabling physical aspects of the environment, but to what Susan Wendell (1996) describes as the perception of disabled people as 'other'. This otherness evokes fears of one's own physical limitations, one's own lack of the 'perfect body' and one's own future loss of abilities leading to death. Wendell notes that society also identifies 'disabled heroes' (Helen Keller, Stephen Hawking, Paralympic competitors), but this merely increases the otherness of most disabled people, since they lack the resources and the physical capacities to 'overcome' their disability in these dramatic ways. Thus, in less obvious ways than in the past perhaps, society may single out disabled people as 'freaks', though such a word might never be used. Wendell summarizes the problem this creates for people who, like her, suffer from an irremediable disability:

they must struggle harder than non-disabled people for a self-image that is both realistic and positive, and this is made more difficult by other people's reactions to them. In a society that idealizes the body, people who cannot come close enough to the ideals, and those whose bodies are out of control, become devalued people because of their devalued bodies. Moreover, they are constant reminders to the temporarily 'normal' of the rejected body – of what the normal are trying to avoid, forget, and ignore.

(Wendell 1996: 91)

There can be no more dramatic illustration of how powerfully rejecting social forces can be than the decision of some parents of Down syndrome children to arrange for surgical reconstruction of their facial features. Such children have (in varying degrees) a set of facial and bodily features, including a distinctive nose and eye shape, which led in the past to them being described as 'mongoloid'. The condition is a chromosomal disorder, and results in a lower than average IQ and (until recently with advances in heart surgery) a significantly lowered life expectancy. There are more enlightened attitudes to people with Down syndrome and much improved educational programmes allowing them to develop their potential (Goeke et al. 2003). However, Down syndrome in children results in fears, at least in some parents, that they will be stigmatized, teased and discriminated against.

Since the 1970s some surgeons have performed plastic surgery, with the consent of parents, in an effort to change the distinctive appearance and so lead to greater acceptance of the children into society. The operations have been performed at an age when the children themselves could not give consent, and have involved major reconstructive work, including reductions in the size of the tongue, implants in the bridge of the nose, cheeks and jawbone, change in the folds of the eyelids, removal of fatty tissue from chin and neck, and ear repositioning (Goeke et al. 2003). It goes without saying that many of these are highly invasive surgical procedures and must have resulted in considerable post-operative pain and discomfort, as well as psychological distress to the children, who would be unable to understand what was happening to them. This all raises the question of whether such interventions can be described in terms of promoting the 'best interests' of the child, especially since all that the surgery does is to mask, not to change, the underlying condition. One commentator has compared it to female circumcision (or genital mutilation), which is carried out for social conformity reasons in some societies, but is outlawed in most Western countries as a form of child abuse (Jones 2000).

In fact the claimed benefit to the child may not be supported by empirical evidence, though the operation may make some parents feel better. Arndt et al. (1986) found that lay raters, shown pre- and post-operative pictures, considered the post-operative appearance to be slightly less attractive, though the parents thought it noticeably improved. A similar result was found by

Klaiman and Arndt (1989) in another study, which used videotapes of conversational speech before and after and adolescent lay raters. Lay raters could not discern any improvements in speech or appearance, though the parents did. Another study found little support for the effectiveness of the operation, even from parents themselves (Kravetz *et al.* 1992). Perhaps the most significant finding is that of Goeke *et al.* (2003). In a survey of 250 parents of children with Down syndrome, they found that 88 per cent were opposed to surgery and only three parents had had it done. The reasons for parental opposition were that this would simply increase prejudice in two ways: first, the cues that would help people understand and recognize the different behaviour of the children would be eliminated, and this could lead to greater intolerance; second, the attempt to conceal the condition would undercut efforts to educate the public about the condition and to change prejudicial attitudes to such children.

Thus we can conclude this section on the rejected body by noting that a surgical solution to a social problem seems far removed from how we would hope that societies can learn to accept differences between people. No one would doubt that plastic surgery to remove defacing physical features (such as growths or birthmarks) or to repair the devastating effects of accidents or burns would be in the best interests of the individuals concerned. But when plastic surgery becomes an attempt to conceal alienated, despised or rejected bodies, a boundary is crossed from medical care to what has been described as 'enhancement surgery'. At times this boundary may be hard to define, but when enduring human characteristics of fragility, mortality and disability are to be hidden behind a fleshly mask, clearly we have lost the ability to tolerate anything that deviates from some external social standard of human goodness and acceptability. Yet again the body has become alien.

The ultimate fashion accessory

As will be evident from the last section, there is a fuzzy boundary between *plastic* (or reconstructive) surgery and *cosmetic or aesthetic*[2] (enhancement) surgery. This mirrors a general debate in medical ethics about the use of medical techniques of all kinds for human enhancement as opposed to therapy for injury or illness. Some would claim that the distinction is a false one, since all medicine aims at betterment and the alleged distinction is just a matter of degree (see, for example, the view of the World Transhumanist Association, www.transhumanism.org). Others see the fundamental aims of medicine as being subverted when it is used merely as a technique for the furtherance of human desire, rather than as a means of overcoming disease and disability. (This debate is well represented in Miller 2006.) This could simply be a debate about appropriate use of public funds for health care, in which case some distinction (however difficult) has to be drawn between medical need and personal desire or preference. But since the vast proportion of cosmetic surgery is paid for privately, the real issue at debate is whether its practitioners have really left the profession of medicine and have become merely highly skilled technicians in the beauty industry.

This is an important debate for those concerned about the nature of professionalism in medicine and the maintenance of professional standards, but, as in earlier sections of this chapter, the focus of our discussion here is elsewhere. For our theme, the interesting question is how, with the current dramatic rise in cosmetic surgery,[3] the body has become what I have called 'the ultimate fashion accessory'. In this ever more popular 'makeover' approach to our bodily shape and external appearance the body has become like a garment, an adornment to be altered and embellished according to the current dictates of fashion. Something strange indeed has happened to the embodied self in the promised land of cosmetic medicine! Now the person ages, but the body remains youthful; the person experiences pain, worry and laughter, but the lineaments of these experiences are wiped away by a medical treatment that smoothes every wrinkle and restricts facial expression to prevent new lines on the skin; mortality, individuality and vulnerability are concealed by the artistry of the purveyors of 'the perfect body'.

Of course, cosmetic alteration of the human body is not a purely modern phenomenon, nor is it restricted to the post-industrial societies in which cosmetic surgery has boomed. Traces of ochre probably used for facial and body painting have been found in pre-historic sites. Reconstruction of noses was practised as early as 600 BC, though in this case to replace ones removed as punishment (Kuczynski 2006: 64). The extraordinary (to Western eyes) alteration of women's bodies by bands extending the neck in the Padaung people, or causing major extension of the pierced lower or upper lip in a number of African tribal traditions, or the excruciating practice of binding women's feet in Chinese tradition, are all well known examples of how women's bodies through the ages have been subjected to cultural hegemony; and changing facial appearance through tattooing (dramatically so in the case of Maori and Pacific Island warriors) provides instances of alteration of the male body for social ends. So is there really anything so new or unusual about the current boom in cosmetic surgery (and other techniques like facial peels and Botox injections) in the wealthier societies of our day?

The answer must be both yes and no. The similarity lies in the obvious effect of social forces in determining how the ideal body is understood. In this respect the tattooed Maori warrior, the officer-class German with duelling scars on his face, and contemporary pop idols with wrinkle free skin and sculpted bodies are really all subjects of the same master – social conformity. However, there is an important difference, and this lies in the rhetoric of freedom, choice and self-realization through which the ministrations of cosmetic medicine are marketed to a mass audience. For here lie profound ironies: conformity has become portrayed as freedom and mere appearance as the true reality.

The power of the image

Cosmetic medicine has moved out of the world of the rich and powerful into a huge mass market. In 2005, 11.5 million surgical and non-surgical cosmetic procedures were performed in the USA; the main professional association has over five thousand members, and there are countless other doctors performing non-surgical procedures such as Botox injections, since all that is required to do this is medical registration (Kuczynski, 2006: 78). With the increase in market demand, the price for the most popular procedures has dropped considerably, and (surprisingly) almost 70 per cent of people having them have incomes of less than US$40,000 per year (Tong and Lindemann 2006: 184). This mass appeal clearly stems from the power of advertising, just in the same way as that of all successfully branded products does. Popular television programmes in the USA (*Extreme Makeover*; *The Swan*; *Queer Eye for the Straight Guy*) have sold to an obese and car-addicted society the idea of a quick (though not painless) solution to their body problems. Moreover, in the States the removal of prohibitions on direct advertising by doctors to the public has opened the way for advertising campaigns targeted at different sections of the population.

Yet being persuaded to buy the latest fashion in shoes, handbags or brand-named outfits is much less of a radical purchasing choice than paying to have invasive, and at times risky and painful, liposuction, Botox injections or enhancement surgery. So, what is the power that sells such products? In her article 'Reading the slender body', Susan Bordo (1998) argues that the current obsession with body shape and bodily appearance generally is related to the anxieties provoked by the contradictions of our consumer culture. She describes the tension as follows:

> On the one hand, as producers of goods and services we must sublimate, delay, repress desires for immediate gratification; we must cultivate the work ethic. On the other hand, as consumers, we must display a boundless capacity to capitulate to desire and indulge in impulse; we must hunger for constant and immediate satisfaction. The regulation of desire thus becomes an ongoing problem, as we find ourselves continually besieged by temptation, while socially condemned for over-indulgence.
>
> (Bordo 1998: 296f.)

In this context the appeal of cosmetic medicine begins to make sense, for what it promises is management of oneself to live successfully in our consumer orientated society. The betrayals by our body – increasing fat, deteriorating looks, worry lines between our eyes, which reveal us as self-indulgent or as social failures – are reversed through diet, exercise and (quickest of all) cosmetic medicine. Now we project a different image, one that conveys that 'one "cares" about oneself and how one appears to others, suggesting will-power, emerging control over infantile impulse, the ability to "shape your life"' (Bordo 1998: 295).

Subjugation or empowerment?

What, then, are we to make of the rising tide of cosmetic medicine? Does it matter that more and more people are being persuaded by the rhetoric of self-improvement to 'shape up' to an image of attractiveness and success by medical and surgical interventions on their bodies? The key issue seems to be whether these trends are any more of a concern than the selling of brands in general, which also works by keying into people's insecurities about their social status and their attractiveness to others. Why is a 'nose job' any different in principle from the skilful application of make-up, or liposuction from weight loss through dieting and exercise, or a breast implant from an 'uplift' brassiere?

Clearly these examples differ in the degree of intrusiveness and also in the permanence of the change, and that may be significant. Put in other terms, we can say that these non-medical interventions do not inscribe on the body the passing whims and prejudices of the current age, as cosmetic surgery does. Nose shapes, for example, are associated with racial prejudice; the boyish body of current female fashion seems to reflect a rejection of the motherly image associated with ample hips; and the fixation with large breasts a particular stereotype of female sexuality. Cosmetic medicine ensures, more drastically and permanently than diets or other beauty treatments do, that the body conforms to the current fashion.

In an interesting article surveying the change in feminist evaluations of cosmetic medicine, Tong and Lindemann (2006) have pointed out that, while previous critiques saw it as part of patriarchal enslavement of women through the imposition of cultural stereotypes of femininity, later writers have suggested that cosmetic surgery and other beauty treatments can be used by women as a means of empowerment and self-affirmation. A good example of the critique of cosmetic medicine can be found in Bartky's book *Femininity and Domination: Studies in the Phenomenology of Oppression* (1990). She writes:

> Women are no longer required to be chaste or modest, to restrict their sphere of activity to the home, or even to realize their properly feminine destiny in maternity. Normative femininity [that is, rules for being a good woman] is coming more and more to be centered on woman's body – not its duties and obligations or even its capacity to bear children, but its sexuality, more precisely, its presumed heterosexuality and its appearance.
>
> (Bartky 1990: 81)

Bartky goes on to compare the resultant experience of women in this social context with that of the prisoners in Bentham's experimental prison, the Pantopticon, which was designed for constant surveillance. Equally, the socially conformist woman has to monitor herself relentlessly to make sure her appearance is always as it should be. Bartky concludes, 'this self-surveillance is a form of obedience to patriarchy' (1990: 80). Thus for Bartky and many other feminist authors of that era (see, for example, Wolf 1991; Bordo 1993; Haiken 1997) resistance to cosmetic medicine was required as part of a more general opposition to the domination of women by cultural stereotypes.

However, later work, which involved interviews with women who had elected to have cosmetic surgery, revealed a different picture. For example, Gimlin (2002) found that many of the women she interviewed did not see themselves as coerced by social stereotypes into seeking a perfect body; rather, they saw the choice of cosmetic surgery as an independent decision, helping them to approximate more closely to how they wanted to be. Similar findings had emerged from the work of Davis (1995), in which she found one feminist friend who did not regard having surgery to enhance her appearance as a betrayal of feminist principles. Rather, she described it as the opportunity 'to renegotiate her relationship to her body and through her body to the world around her' (quoted in Tong and Lindemann 2006: 188).

Thus some later feminist writers see cosmetic medicine as potentially empowering. Accepting that sexist norms and stereotypes can be degrading and disempowering, they believe that women can consciously turn this potential repression into a form of liberation. This can mean aggressively displaying their femininity and so making 'a sexual statement that was powerful rather than passive' (Karp and Stoller 1999, quoted in Tong and Lindemann 2006: 191); or using their conformity to the stereotypes of attractiveness to negotiate a more influential position in society, thus turning an oppressing power into an enabling one. It is interesting to note that one of the pioneers of cosmetic surgery, Dr Suzanne Noël, who operated in the early decades of last century and wrote one of the first textbooks on the topic, saw this as her *raison d'être* – by operating on women to delay the effects of ageing or to improve their appearance she believed she was enabling them to retain their jobs or obtain better ones (see Davis 1999). It is also notable that Dr Noël was a woman surgeon, in an era when this was virtually unknown.

Appearance and reality

How, then, should we evaluate cosmetic medicine in terms of its overall contribution to our perception of ourselves as *embodied* selves? Does it reinforce demeaning and deceptive cultural stereotypes (the myths of the perfect body and of everlasting youth); or does it merely demonstrate the malleability of the human body, providing us with choices for re-invention of the self not available to previous generations? Bordo, in an essay entitled

'Normalization and resistance in an era of the image' (1997), seems to provide the most satisfactory answer to this question. Basing her analysis on the work of Jean Baudrillard (1983), she describes our post-modern era as one in which the distinction between reality and appearance has ceased to carry any weight, for 'all that is meaningful to us are our simulations' (Bordo 1997: 451). Using the pop star Cher as her example, she points out that although Cher's extraordinarily youthful image has to be a fabricated one, given her chronological age, it has all the force of reality for those who admire her. Indeed, far from seeming to be a victim of cultural oppression, Cher conveys a powerful message of individuality, of resistance to convention and of liberated self-invention, very similar to another popular female icon, Madonna. In the case of both of these world famous entertainers, the constructed image *is* the reality so far as the audience is concerned. Moreover, as techniques of computer simulation become more and more sophisticated, we are surrounded by things we know to be fabricated, yet which come across to us as reality. So, in our age, the human body itself has become simply a medium for images. Bordo sums this up as follows:

> our relationship to physical appearance ... has come to be understood not as a biological 'given' which we have to learn to accept, but as plastic potentiality to be pressed into the service of image – to be arranged, re-arranged, constructed and deconstructed as we choose.
>
> (Bordo 1997: 452)

These observations by Bordo call to mind the popular movie *The Matrix*, in which it is revealed that what seems like reality is in fact a set of simulations created by a vast computer wired up to incubated humans. A similar theme is explored by the movie *The Truman Show*, in which the main character discovers that what he thought was the real world is in fact a huge TV studio populated by actors producing a popular soap opera. It is perhaps significant that in both these movies the 'good' characters struggle to break out of the simulated world, despite its apparent harmony and perfection.

Applying this to cosmetic medicine, we find the basis for a different sort of critique from that offered by the early feminists. Cosmetic medicine may well contribute to an illusion of consumer 'choice', since that alleged choice is in fact manipulated by a highly effective advertising industry. But in this respect, our critique has to extend to the whole beauty and fashion industry. It may well bolster sexist and patriarchal attitudes to women, but again this is no different from the industry as a whole. On the other side of the equation, we have seen how it could be used to gain power rather than be victimized by it. It may well help some people (both men and women) to overcome unhappiness with their bodily appearance, give them more self-confidence and perhaps contribute to success in work or personal relationships. So if we try to assess it by its likely short-term results, we cannot credibly single out cosmetic medicine from the whole apparatus of branding and the selling of fashion trends. But the deeper question is whether its focus on radically altering the shape and appearance of the body – the *sculpting* of the body, as the industry describes it – is contributing to our loss of contact with the body as a living, changing and (finally) dying organism. If the body is to become no more than the repository of images of how we would like life to be, we cannot in fact live truly human lives at all, since we are trying to escape the realities of ageing and death. Yet, surely human beauty is to be found in living, changing and dying bodies, not in some unchanging artefact of the fashion industry. It is to the beauty of the unbranded body that we finally turn – I call it the 'fragility of beauty'.

The fragility of beauty

The poet Robert Shannon has written about beauty in terms of a contrast between the living and the plastic flower:[4]

> How exquisite and how perfect is the living flower which knows both birth and dying:
> While the plastic flower which lasts a thousand years is ever brutal in its changelessness.
>
> (Shannon 1975)

Shannon's poetry conveys the centrality of vulnerability and mortality in any understanding of human beauty. Yet we are in very contentious territory here! Concepts of beauty and ugliness are notoriously subjective and culturally bound. We need merely think of portrayals of the female figure in the artworks and popular cultures of different eras – contrast the classical proportions of the Venus de Milo with the ample curves in *Venus Rising from the Waves* by Botticelli and the sylphlike figures of Beardsley's Art Nouveau, to pick merely a few examples. Equally, the pop female images of our own era show sharp contrasts – compare the ample, 'hour-glass' figures of Diana Dors, Gina Lollobrigida or Marilyn Monroe with the trim, almost boyish figures of Cher or (the older) Jane Fonda. Moreover, many theoreticians of art have questioned whether 'beauty', however understood, really has a place in the understanding of art. For example, Stolnitz starts an essay on the history of the idea of beauty as follows: 'We have to catch ourselves up in order to recognize that "beauty" has receded or even disappeared from contemporary aesthetic theory. For, like other influential ideas, it has simply faded away' (1961: 185).

Danto (2002), in his discussion of 'the abuse of beauty', makes a similar point, tracing the demise of the use of the concept to the aesthetic theory of the 1960s and onwards. He suggests that the reason for this is that representational art has largely been rejected in favour of purely expressive art, and that 'no constraints govern the way visual works of art should look. An artwork can look like anything, and be made of anything – anything is possible' (Danto 2002: 35). A consequence of this is that there is no point in seeing beauty as essential to art. It could not 'be part of the definition of art, if anything can be an artwork, since it is certainly not true that anything can be beautiful' (Danto 2002: 36). Danto concludes his essay with this appraisal of where beauty belongs in a contemporary understanding of the power and importance of art:

> Beauty is one mode among many through which thoughts are presented in art to human sensibility – disgust, horror, sublimity, and sexuality are still others. These modes explain the relevance of art to human existence, and room for them all must be found in an adequate definition of art.
>
> (Danto 2002: 56)

It is notable that Danto does not reject the notion of some kind of objective beauty, which may transcend cultural and historical differences in taste: he merely accepts that we cannot use the concept of the beautiful as the arbiter of artistic worth. Rather, art serves to move us in different ways, some of which may be a response to the sublimely beautiful; others could be a response to human realities, which might appear ugly to most observers. He quotes as an example of the latter the appreciation of the power of Mantegna's Simone Madonna by the art critic Robert Fry, with reference to the artist's portrayal of the infant Jesus: 'The wizened face, the creased and crumpled flesh of a new born babe ... all the penalty, the humiliation, almost the squalor attendant upon "being made flesh" are marked' (Danto 2002: 45).

How, then, are we to understand the claims of the cosmetic medicine industry to be responding to 'aesthetic' norms if such claims cannot even be accurately related to creative art in our era? As I suggested earlier, we must surely see these claims to be no more than a reflection of our contemporary capture by the power of the image, to the extent that we no longer perceive any other reality. We may return to the analysis of our post-modern world by Baudrillard, to appreciate the depth of this problem:

> So art is everywhere, since artifice lies at the heart of reality. So art is dead, since not only is its critical transcendence dead, but reality itself, entirely impregnated by an aesthetic that holds onto its very structurality, has become inseparable from its own image.
>
> (Baudrillard 1993: 75)

Baudrillard gives as a potent example of this transformation the celebrated Andy Warhol reiterative portrayal of Marilyn Monroe: 'the multiple replicas of Marilyn Monroe's face are of course at the same time the death of the original and the end of representation' (Baudrillard 1993: 69).

So what more can be said? Just that this is our age, where the image is all? Certainly Baudrillard, in a set of lectures given just before the beginning of the new millennium, paints an apocalyptic picture of what awaits us, now that our whole world is simulation:

> Thus, freedom has been obliterated, liquidated by liberation; truth has become supplanted by verification; the community has been liquidated and absorbed by communication; form gives way to information and performance. Everywhere we see a paradoxical logic: the idea is destroyed by its own realization, by its own excess. And in this way history itself comes to an end, finds itself obliterated by the instantaneity and omnipresence of the event.
>
> (Baudrillard and Witwer 2000: 47)

We may see these predictions as extreme, yet the omnipresence of image and its threat to those things we treasure in our humanity can scarcely be denied. Cosmetic medicine presents us with a fundamentally deceptive picture of what it means to be human, in which beauty is portrayed as a purchasable product, an artefact. Worse, it seems to suggest that somehow by conforming to these images we will find fulfilment in our lives. In his wise and witty critique of American medicine and American values, *Better than Well*, Carl Elliott has captured the remorseless logic behind the beauty industry:

> The problem is not just that certain people's looks don't meet the standards of the culture, but also that the underlying social structures demand so much of self-presentation. In America, your social status is tied to your self-presentation, and if your self-presentation fails, then your status drops. If your status drops, then so does your self-respect. Without self-respect you cannot be truly fulfilled. If you are not fulfilled, you are not living a truly meaningful life.
>
> (Elliott 2003: 205)

I fear that Elliott's critique applies far more universally than to America alone. Against this false picture of how fulfilment is to be found, we must assert the essential fragility of human beauty, something discovered in the lights and shadows of our life together as changing, vulnerable and mortal beings. Our shared experiences of birth, intimacy and death are where hope of a human future, however uncertain, is to be found. This is the 'beauty that binds', rather than the beauty that divides us from one another in a hopeless race to be the best (or at least not amongst the worst). For these reasons we must be profoundly concerned about the rise of cosmetic medicine, not only for its potential harm to some individuals, but for its contribution to the loss of our shared humanity, as profoundly varied and changing individual selves.

Conclusion: the body and its discontents

In this chapter we have surveyed the many ways in which human beings experience the discomfort of embodiment. Some of this discontent seems to originate from within the person, as with the transsexual, persons with BIID or with eating disorders, who experience an innate 'wrongness' in their bodies; some is imposed upon the person by the society, as with the rejection experienced by persons with physical disability or the child with Down syndrome, 'shielded' from prejudice by facial surgery. Much of the discontent seems to originate from a mixture of personal factors and social forces, as people internalize powerful social images of ideal sexuality, or perfect body shape, or 'true beauty', or eternal youth.

Can we escape from this discontent? This seems unlikely, for the whole impetus to production and consumption which drives post-industrial societies depends on maintaining a sense of dissatisfaction with one's current state. The beauty industry is hardly likely to change its marketing policies on the basis of the poverty of the values it promotes! (However, it is notable that concern about anorexia in young women has led to the fashion industry in Italy and France controlling the extremes of thinness in its models.) One might, of course, look for radical alternatives, rejecting outright the deceptive images which fuel consumer demand. An interesting example of this can be found in the 'A manifesto for cyborgs', written by Donna Haraway (1991). Haraway seeks to break away totally from the limits 'proposed by the mundane fiction of Man and Woman' (1991: 524). She finds the imagery in feminist science fiction depicting cyborgs – a mixture of human and machine. In this imagery gender stereotypes are finally broken and the cyborg can make and celebrate its own reality:

> The machine is us, our processes, an aspect of our embodiment ... female embodiment seemed to be given organic necessity ... Cyborgs might consider more seriously the partial, fluid, sometimes aspect of sex and embodiment. Gender might not be global identity after all, even if it has profound historical breadth and depth.
>
> (Haraway 1991: 524–25)

The force of Haraway's depiction of such cyborg values comes from its refusal to accept any of the basic assumptions about the nature of humans and human sexuality, which we all take for granted. This is, of course, a heuristic device. She does not have to prove that such a radical alteration of human nature is any more than speculative, science fictional. The point is that she can challenge assumptions about how human life *must* be, with the hypothesis of a being over whom the images of gendered marketing could have no influence. This device frees us from the deceptions of beauty, sexual attractiveness and social success on which the market depends.

A less radical solution might be simply to be willing to live with difference and diversity in our human embodiments, rejecting the myth of the perfect, unchangeable body in favour of the celebration of the myriad forms in which human life is experienced. We need to fight prejudice against those whose bodies are perceived as inferior because they deviate from some totally arbitrary social norm of attractiveness. We need to see the wide spectrum of gender difference, and avoid the polarization of male and female, with its associated stereotyped social roles. Above all, we need to restore ageing and death to the appropriate place in the journey of each human life. The ultimate deception of the funeral home viewing of the dead is graphically described by Baudrillard. It attempts to make the dead person retain the appearance of life:

> he still smiles at you, the same colours, the same skin, he seems himself even after death, he is even a little fresher than when he was alive, and lacks only speech. A faked death, idealized in the colours of life: the secret idea is that life is natural and death is against nature. Death must therefore be *naturalized* in a stuffed simulacrum of life.
>
> (Baudrillard 1993: 181)

Instead of this farcical denial of how death is integral to life, we need to help people to live with the losses which being alive inevitably entails – the loss of capacities in ageing, the loss of those dear to you as the years go on, finally the loss of life itself, as one's own death approaches. If we can learn to accept and respect our embodied selves, in all their transitoriness, beauty can be found in unexpected places, and it need not be fabricated or made to last for ever. Shakespeare evokes this human experience of enduring beauty:

> And Time that gave doth now his gift confound.
> Time doth transfix the flourish set on youth
> And delves the parallels in beauty's brow,
> Feeds on the rarities of nature's truth,
> And nothing stands but for his scythe to mow:
> And yet to times in hope, my verse shall stand
> Praising thy worth, despite his cruel hand.
>
> (Shakespeare, *Sonnets,* LX)

Chapter 6

Gifts from the dead

We return finally to the synergy between life and death that constitutes human life as we know it. Because we are mortal, we know both intimacy and grief, both vulnerability and the strength to recover from loss. Knowledge of the certainty of our own death and of the death of those we love shapes our plans, hopes and fears. Of course it is possible to speculate about some technologically engineered human future in which ageing and death are postponed, or even abolished altogether (Post and Binstock 2004).[1] But Baudrillard and Witwer are surely right in seeing this as a kind of nightmare:

> Contrary to everything that seems obvious and 'natural', nature's first creatures were immortal. It was only by obtaining the power to die, by dint of constant struggle, that we became the living beings we are today. Blindly we dream of overcoming death through immortality, when all the time immortality is the most horrific of all fates.
>
> (Baudrillard and Witwer 2000: 6)

We have seen how the denial of ageing and death has led to the illusory world of cosmetic medicine. If, instead, we learn to live with death as a natural part of life, then our feelings about the bodies of the dead can change from fear and disgust to acceptance and gratitude. This could seem somewhat macabre. Harris, in discussing the retained organs controversy, regards reverence for bodily remains as 'quite absurd, if understandable', pointing out that the human body inevitably disintegrates soon after death and 'may end as the bung in a beer barrel or the mortar in a wall' (Harris 2002: 547). Of course this is obviously true, unless (as we shall see later in the chapter) our bodies are plastinated or otherwise preserved. But Harris – perhaps wilfully – misses the point. The corpse of a person we have loved carries a special meaning for most of us. Why else do the families of soldiers killed in action, or of people lost in air crashes, long to be re-united with whatever remains can be found? People do not have illusions about their relatives defeating the decay that comes to all dead organisms, but they do hope for the *physical* reality of disposing reverently of all that remains of the person they loved.

How, then, can we adequately understand the nature of our relationship with the bodies of the dead? I shall consider first 'dishonouring the dead', discussing the controversy over the retention of organs after post mortem examinations and the debate provoked by Gunther von Hagens's travelling exhibition *Body Worlds*. Then I shall discuss ways in which we can feel gratitude to the dead for what they give us: gratitude for the gift of knowledge, the gift of life and the gift of memories.

Dishonouring the dead

The retained organs controversy

In Chapter 1 I described the reactions of the parents of a child whose body parts (including her tongue) were retained after a port mortem examination by a pathologist at Alder Hey Children's Hospital, Liverpool. In their testimony to the public enquiry at Liverpool, the parents described the hospital and the pathologist as 'predators'. Similar language was used by other parents and relatives at meetings of the Retained Organs Commission, a body set up by the UK Government to manage the aftermath of the inquiries in Liverpool and in Bristol. Pathologists were called 'butchers' and the unauthorized removal of babies' hearts and of many other organs was compared with the holocaust.[2] In addition to the Inquiries in Bristol and in Liverpool, another investigation revealed the post mortem removal and storage of brains from patients suffering from mental illness (the Isaacs Report (HM Inspector of Anatomy 2003)). The Retained Organs Commission, tasked with discovering the extent of the storage of retained organs and tissue in England and Wales, estimated that at least 105,000 organs, body parts, still births and foetuses were stored in NHS facilities. Hospital Trusts had received over 30,000 enquiries from families seeking to locate stored organs or tissue (Retained Organs Commission 2002). These figures clearly demonstrate that concern about retention was not limited to just a few families, or to places where the public inquiries had been carried out.

However, some commentators have described the reactions of families to the discovery of retained organs as emotionally excessive, and regard steps to prevent recurrence of such practices (which led to a new Human Tissue Act in England and Wales) as potentially endangering medical progress (Harris 2002). At the same time the medical community, especially the pathologists, who had in good faith followed accepted practices in storing tissue and other body parts removed at post mortem, felt unfairly stigmatized:

> We were made to feel like criminals. I felt awful, absolutely awful ...
> because we were so out of touch with what the general public thought –

apparently – and yet we were doing nothing that we hadn't seen all our colleagues teach us to do.

You know we were told it was a good thing to keep organs, and to do this and to do that. And to find that this was something, that this was something people were getting death threats for was a terrible shock.

(Campbell *et al.* 2008: 105)

Concerns for the future of pathology, as well as for cadaveric organ donation, were voiced in *The Times*:

The body parts furore triggered an irrational and emotional backlash against pathology and organ donation, the effects of which are still being felt. A recent survey published in *New Scientist* found that one in ten pathology posts is vacant, as doctors shy away from joining a profession so widely caricatured as ghoulish.

(*The Times*, 6 December 2003, cited in Seale *et al.* 2005)

So what went wrong in the communication between the medical profession and those families, who had to undergo through the second trauma of discovering that the body that had earlier been subjected to a post mortem had been returned to them incomplete? To the pathologists this was simply normal practice, and their lack of information to the relatives was seen as justified beneficence. But for many families the removal of body parts without their knowledge or consent was seen as a brutal violation of the person they loved and mourned.

In *Doctors' Stories* Kathryn Hunter describes what she calls the 'narrative incommensurability' of doctors' and patients' accounts of illness:

The patient's account of illness and the medical version of that account are fundamentally, irreducibly different narratives, and this difference is essential to the work of medical care. Sick people who seek a physician's advice and help are in quest of exactly this difference, for, physicians are believed not only to know more about the body but also to see its disorders clearly and without shame. Yet because it is scarcely acknowledged by either patient or physician, the difference between their accounts of the patient's malady can warp understanding between them.

(Hunter 1991: 123)

As we see from this quotation, Hunter is not deploring the fact that the narratives are incommensurable – she sees this as necessary for medicine to offer help to the patient. But things go wrong when the difference between the narratives is not acknowledged and understood, and this wrong is compounded when, as in the retained organs controversy, the medical narrative persists past the point where it is either necessary or useful.

Let us compare, then, the way relatives saw the retention of organs after post mortem examination with how it was conceptualized by some of the professional bodies who gave evidence to the Chief Medical Officer's Summit on Organ Retention. The evidence of relatives is fully available in the Inquiry Reports of Bristol and Alder Hey (Bristol Royal Infirmary Inquiry 2000; Royal Liverpool Children's Inquiry 2001). I can give only a few brief excerpts to convey the profound feelings experienced by many families:

> You relive the moment that she died over and over again. I have flash-backs of what they have done and what you imagine they have done. I had a dream the other day that I said to someone in the hospital where I work what is in the cupboard? When we opened it there were three jars: one with babies hearts, one with babies lungs and one, which looked like peas. When I looked closer they were eyes ... I have a great big empty void inside.
>
> She did not know what had happened to her daughter or that she had been desecrated. Alexandra had been stripped bare of everything and someone believed they had the right to do it and to return her apparently complete for funeral purposes but in fact without her organs. For five years she believed Alexandra was intact and at rest.
>
> His parents buried him ten years ago as a shell. It is like grave robbing before being put in the grave. His body had been mutilated.

Compare this testimony from relatives with some of the written evidence given by professional medical associations to the summit meeting called by the Chief Medical Officer of England (Chief Medical Officer's Summit on Organ Retention 2001):

> The fact that in the past many families have not been informed in detail about what a post mortem examination entails ... invariably reflected a simple and understandable wish to spare them further anguish and distress at the time of bereavement.
>
> (Royal College of Pathologists, ref. 101)

> It is perhaps a paradox that in an age when we have more understanding than ever before of the nature of human life and the biology of the human body, we are more distressed than at any time in human history about what is perceived as inappropriate disposal of the whole human body or part of it ... This is a philosophical puzzle.
>
> (President, Royal College of Paediatrics and Child Health, ref. 119)

Perhaps this last quotation is the most powerful indication of the narrative dissonance of the medical and lay understandings of the body. The President of the Royal College of Paediatrics and Child Health could not understand how, with such improved knowledge of the *biology* of the body, relatives can feel distressed when they discover that they have buried a body 'stripped of organs'.

It would be naïve to suppose that these different ways of viewing the human dead body can easily be reconciled. Indeed there may be no need to do so, provided we understand that they serve different purposes, and provided the feelings of the bereaved are properly respected. The medical discourse is functional for achieving the goals of scientific medicine, in which the body-as-object is required in order to create the generalizations that allow for differential diagnosis and (some kinds of) therapeutic intervention. But even in the realm of the living, it is now well recognized that such distancing and objectifying of the body has detrimental effects on health, and offers only limited scope for effective recovery from illness.

When medicine extends uncritically into the realm of the dead and supposes that 'this malformed and damaged heart' (to be stored in a jar for further study) is the same as 'my child's heart' (soon to be buried with my child's body), then it loses the plot completely. The meanings attributed to the parts of the body, by doctors and by the lay public, are in reality completely different, and each has its own rationality. Intimate relationships never concern merely a meeting of minds or of Lockean self-valuing pools of consciousness! The physical body of the person loved is fully part of the love that parent feels for child or wife for husband. This embodiment of the person does not suddenly disappear in death, though, of course, it soon becomes necessary to let go of the body and live only with the memory and mental images of the person now dead. A mother cuddling her dead child, a husband kissing the cold brow of his wife's dead body, are not acts which *deny* the death of the person. They are part of the story of human lives shared and of the pain which comes from parting.

On the other hand, we have to avoid the kind of demonization of the medical profession which emerged from some of the meetings organized by the Retained Organs Commission. Describing pathologists as 'butchers', hospitals as 'predators' and comparing the organ retention regime to the holocaust reveals the depth of anger and grief experienced by some (though by no means all) of the affected relatives. But, in fact, virtually all the health care professionals involved acted out of genuine concern for the families, and, as the following quotation from a pathologist illustrates, were by no means cut off from ordinary human emotions:

> I've done some paediatric autopsy and you know the thing is if you see an old person lying on a slab they look as if they belong there. If ... there's a kid lying in a babygrow, with a teddy bear, they don't look as if they belong on the slab. And you have to take the teddy bear out of their arms, and their baby-grow off, and take off their nappy. And so doing that autopsy is hellish.
>
> (Campbell *et al.* 2008: 106)

Here we see the humanity of the doctor, as she struggles to carry out a pro-fessional role which demands the ability to put feelings aside and perform tasks which few people would find easy. It is becoming better recognized now than it was in the past that medicine can create considerable stress on prac-titioners, and that both addiction rates and suicide rates are higher than the population norms. Consider the following description by a young practi-tioner of how the demands of her work as a junior doctor made her neglect her own body and her own illness:

> There wasn't time to think, there wasn't time to ... be compassionate, you didn't have time to get to know people, you were running physically to keep up ... I knew I had asthma, but I didn't realize that's what was doing it and I couldn't understand why I felt exhausted all the time ... I felt numb, I did feel distanced from my own body ... I think you become less human. And you didn't expect to see yourself as human.
>
> (Jaye 2004: 44)

Thus the dualism that underlies the scientific aspects of medicine begins to infect the personal lives of practitioners, and they can lose sight of both their own feelings and those of patients and their families. A parent giving evi-dence to the Bristol Inquiry describes the effects of the failures of the people dealing with her to tell her the full story of what had been done to her son:

> If only people had been honest and open with parents. I realize that doctors have to be trained and only see organs as specimens. The dis-tress which we have all felt could have been alleviated by treating parents and patients as human beings rather than an extension of specimens.
>
> (quoted in Bristol Royal Infirmary Inquiry 2000)

Yet is it really a fair and balanced judgment to class the actions of those involved in the retention of organs as an example of 'dishonouring the dead'? Clearly many families saw it that way, as I have demonstrated above. But surely the pathologists and the hospitals involved were merely carrying out their duty, in most cases as required by law, since the vast majority of the organ retention cases were the outcome of coronial autopsies. Moreover, the Coroners' Rules governing these autopsies and the 1961 Human Tissue Act (which would have applied to retention after elective post mortems) were sufficiently ambiguous to make the common practice of storage and retention of organs and tissue understandable, though of 'dubious legality' (Brazier 2002; see also Skegg 1991).[3] In addition, coronial autopsies and other post mortem examinations are of obvious benefit to society, both in assisting the application of criminal justice and in gaining a better understanding of the effectiveness of therapies and the causes of death. One pathologist argues strongly that his work is a form of altruism:

My own viewpoint is that I do my job for the benefit of society and that autopsy is a form of altruism. Well, I know that half the people in the street would not hold that – they would hold the ethical position that the body belongs to the parents and the parents have an absolute right to decide what is done with it because it's a private issue. I don't think autopsy is a private issue, I think it's too important, I think it's very much a public issue.

(quoted in Campbell *et al.* 2008: 105)

So, what might it mean to say that the dead are dishonoured? After all, there are plenty of clear historical examples of deliberately besmirching the reputation of the dead and of holding them in contempt. The bodies of criminals, especially those convicted of acts of treason against the Crown, would be hung, drawn and quartered and their heads put on spikes for public display; moreover, when suicide was regarded as both a sin and a crime, the bodies of the 'culprits' would be buried at crossroads with sharp flints on top of them, symbolizing the eternal pains of hell they were thought to endure. How can we compare the retention of organs and tissue to such deliberate acts of public disgrace?

Of course, there can be no valid comparison here. But we need to return to the problem of the disjunction between scientific medicine and lay understandings of the body to appreciate why unauthorized organ removal and retention was seen by the families as a violation of the dignity and integrity of the person they loved. To the medical scientist, organs removed from a dead body are primarily sources of information. Were they to be confused with the reality of the person now dead, a pathologist could hardly be expected to carry out her work. Preserving and storing such material for further testing and research, or slicing it into thin wafers to make into microscopic slides, is simply part of good practice, and can be rightly seen as routine. However, to the relatives of the dead person, such a disaggregation of the parts of the body is hard to accept and understand. (Thus parents spoke of being given – without their knowledge – the 'empty shell' of their child to bury.) Moreover, some body parts carry powerful symbolic significance for the grieving relatives – the brain, the heart, the tongue, the eyes, the hands and the sexual organs.[4] Thus one parents' group named itself 'Stolen Hearts'; and the parents of a child who had struggled to learn to speak were particularly distressed to hear that her tongue had been removed and retained. The point is that, for grieving relatives, body parts *are* personal. Although the person they loved is dead, the body is still treasured as the locus of the uniqueness they have lost – *my* child's heart is not just any heart! We can see this clearly in the distress caused to the widow of an orthodox Jew who had committed suicide when his body was removed from her house and subjected to a coronial autopsy. The following excerpts are taken from Mrs Isaacs's account given to the inquiry by the HM Inspector of Anatomy into these events:

On finally going into my lounge I was to see what would be the para-
medics carrying something downstairs. I then realized it was my late
husband's body. I asked what was happening and they said the body was
being removed to a mortuary as there would have to be a post mortem. I
said I did not want my husband's body removing, that we were Jewish
and in my mind I knew there were many things because of our faith, for
instance my husband should be going to a Jewish mortuary. Also my
husband should have had someone sat with him during the night namely
a Jewish person ...

I was not asked – I was told – that the body had to be taken out of
the house and that there would be a post mortem on the following Monday.
My husband had died on the Thursday evening. Jewish law states clearly
that burial of the whole body must take place within 24 hours of death.

(quoted in HM Inspector of Anatomy 2003)

Subsequently Mrs Isaacs discovered that her husband's brain had been
retained, so in fact he was not buried whole. In *Speaking for the Dead* Gareth
Jones (2000) recounts another example of retention of a brain against the
wishes of the deceased person, a young man, Timothy Stride, killed in a road
accident, who had clearly stated previously, in a discussion about organ
donation, that he wanted 'to leave this world intact'. His mother described
her continuing sense of failure to honour his wishes when she discovered two
years after cremation that his brain had been removed. She said: 'It was my
son's heart and brain that made him what he was and I am sure most parents would feel the same' (quoted in Jones 2000: 10). We also see a similar
equation of an organ with the essence of the person in the testimony of a
parent to the Bristol Inquiry: 'If they had asked us whether they could retain
Lewis's heart for whatever reason we would have said no because we believe
that the heart is the soul of the person' (quoted in Bristol Royal Infirmary
Inquiry 2000).

In the last analysis, there will always be a balance to be found between, on
the one hand, societal interests in having an effective autopsy system which
meets the needs of accurate diagnosis and the promotion of medical research
and, on the other hand, the concerns of individuals that they and their relatives are treated with dignity and respect after death. John Harris claims that
'the complaint of those who object to actions that violate the physical
integrity of the corpse is scarcely rational' (2002: 527), and he would like to
see the courts and the state not giving these priority when human welfare is
at stake. Margot Brazier, in her response to Harris and in a later article on
consent in the context of organ contention, draws on her experience as Chair
of the Retained Organs Commission to stress the reasonableness of the
reactions of relatives to unauthorized removal and retention. She points to
the 'overwhelming importance for the health and future of that family' that
the remains of family members are disposed in a manner that respects their

religious or personal beliefs. Otherwise their grief is compounded by a sense of betrayal, that they (albeit unwittingly) let their relative down, since 'they failed to safeguard his and their fundamental values' (Brazier 2003: 32).

To honour the dead is certainly only partly connected to the way we treat their bodies, but it cannot be right to suppose that their mortal remains are to be valued as no more than (swiftly decaying) meat. I have been arguing throughout this book that to ignore the bodily aspects of ourselves, or to treat them in a merely instrumental way as a source of income or of social esteem, is ultimately threatening to the integrity of ourselves as individuals and as members of a human community. Ruth Richardson, in *Death, Dissection and the Destitute*, sums it up well: 'What is done to the dead ... is done to us all' (1987: 427).

Displaying the dead body

The retained organs controversy provides an example of dealing with dead bodies in a way that ignores the consent or wishes of deceased persons or their families. But what of uses of the body to which the person may have consented, but which cause offence to others? Over the past decade the German anatomist Gunther von Hagens has created controversy from his public display of plastinated human corpses, called *Body Worlds* (*Körperwelten*). The exhibition (which is open to the general public for an entry fee) has now toured over 40 countries in Asia, Europe and North America, and has been viewed by more than 25 million people (statistics are available from the website (see the website of *Body Worlds* at http://www.bodyworlds.com/en/exhibitions/current_exhibitions.html#BW_Europe). In 2002 von Hagens created further controversy by carrying out the first public autopsy in the UK for over 200 years. This took place before a selected (paying) audience in London, and an edited version of it was broadcast later that night on the terrestrial television channel Channel 4 (Miah and Rich 2008). Shortly, I shall discuss the ethical issues which have been raised about these public displays of preserved dead bodies and of anatomical dissection, but first we should note that – apart from the technique of plastination, which was invented by von Hagens himself – there is nothing new about these events. The 'father' of modern anatomy, Andreas Vesalius (1514–64), carried out public dissections in his 'Theatre of Anatomy' in Brussels (Morriss-Kay 2002) – and the term 'anatomy *theatre*' persists to this day. It was only with the regulation of medicine and of anatomical dissection in the nineteenth century that cadaveric dissection became confined to medical schools and to trainee health professionals (Jones 2000). So far as the display of preserved corpses is concerned, there are, of course, innumerable examples from the past and the present, including the 'auto-icon' of the founder of Utilitarianism, Jeremy Bentham, in University College, London and of Lenin in his mausoleum in Moscow.[5] The von Hagens display, however, is significantly different, as the bodies are placed in 'artistic' poses and are partly dissected to reveal the details of the anatomy.

The technique of plastination was introduced by von Hagens in the late 1970s and has become widely used in anatomy departments mainly as an adjunct to the teaching of gross anatomy (Jones 2002). There is now an International Society for Plastination and a journal associated with it. Barilan describes the process as follows:

> it allows for the first time in history, to transform dead tissue into a colorful, odorless and durable material. In the first stage, a traditionally dissected specimen is frozen and all its fat and water are replaced with acetone. Then acetone is vacuumed out and replaced by plastic resins. The final product is about 80% plastic and 20% organic. From a practical point of view, a plastinized object feels, smells and behaves just like plastic. It looks, though, like genuine human tissue.
>
> (Barilan 2006: 234)

In *Body Worlds* von Hagens has used this technique to present displays of bodies and parts of bodies in many dramatic poses. Examples include a chess playing scene, a rider and horse, a figure holding his own flayed skin (similar to the figure of St Bartholomew in the Sistine Chapel fresco of the Last Judgment), and a pregnant woman with the foetus in her womb also preserved and fully visible. Reactions to the displays range from admiration and awe to disgust and condemnation. For example, one viewer of the first exhibition in London in 2002 gave it the highest praise in her review in the *Journal of Anatomy*:

> The revealed brain, spinal cord and spinal nerves of the sitting "Chess Player" cannot be bettered by anything I have seen as a teaching aid of these structures for medical students. The gigantic masterpiece of the horse and its partially duplicated rider perhaps combine anatomical information with artistic creativity. But most of all, the sheer beauty of the human body is displayed here, in a manner that is a joy to see.
>
> (Morriss-Kay 2002: 536)

On the other hand, religious and civil authorities have in some places sought to prevent or censor aspects of the displays, on the grounds of offences to public decency or to human dignity. Some aspects of the exhibits have also been seen as potentially harmful to at least some visitors. An anatomist, in a letter to *Clinical Anatomy*, described 'a huge number of newborn malformations and still born children piled on a multistory cake', which not only shocked him personally, but could have caused much distress to pregnant women visiting the exhibit (Weiglein 2002). Questions have also been raised about the sources of some of the bodies used by von Hagens. Barilan (2006) quotes a claim that he received a consignment of 56 corpses from the Medical Academy of Novosibirsk, which may have included prisoners, homeless people and psychiatric patients. Von Hagens himself confirms that some bodies came from donations by the family or the dead person and others were from existing collections and could include 'unclaimed bodies'. His organization now clearly favours voluntary donations, and full information is available on the website, as well as at the exhibits themselves, where donor cards can be filled out. Clearly, however, not all exhibits can have been with consent of the dead individual, for example the foetus in the pregnant woman's uterus and the stillborn babies.

In a careful analysis of the ethics of *Body Worlds*, Jones (2002) has pointed out the ambiguity of its portrayal of the dead. It could be seen as art, education or simply entertainment. Von Hagens himself has in the past offered various terms to describe what he is doing: 'anatomy art' (in the catalogue of the exhibition in 2000); and 'edutainment' (in an earlier version of the website, referenced by Lozanoff (2002)). Jones concludes that the exhibition is ethically unacceptable 'if it amounts to little more than entertainment, if it exploits human beings (both living and dead), and if the donations lack truly informed consent'. On the other hand, if the consent is adequate and the exhibits are of genuine use for education and research, then Jones sees the work of von Hagens as an exciting way of bringing the insights of anatomy back into public space (Jones 2002: 439).

So are the dead dishonoured by such public displays? Is von Hagens a 'scientist or a showman' (Singh 2003)? Jones is surely right to say that this all depends on what the genuine purpose of the exhibition is. If it is really just a modern, sophisticated version of the nineteenth-century fondness for freak shows, then it does not matter that the anonymity of the donors is protected or that they have given fully informed consent. We degrade ourselves and the dead by using their dissected bodies for voyeuristic ends. Von Hagens himself strongly contests the criticism that what he is doing is no more than showmanship. In the latest version of the *Body Worlds* website he makes very high claims for what the exhibition can achieve:

> The presentation of the pure physical reminds visitors to BODY WORLDS of the intangible and the unfathomable. The plastinated post-mortal body illuminates the soul by its very absence.
>
> Plastination transforms the body, an object of individual mourning, into an object of reverence, enlightenment, and appreciation.
>
> I hope for BODY WORLDS to be a place of enlightenment and contemplation, even of philosophical and religious self-recognition.
>
> (see prelude to the website, www.bodyworlds.com)

So here we have a claim that stresses honour not dishonour for the dead body. As well as helping the visitors to the exhibition to appreciate the beauty of the structures of the human body, the plastinated corpses open a door to contemplation, helping people see their own mortality. Mourning is transformed into enlightenment.

Such claims are by their nature impossible to prove or disprove. It seems likely that visitors will experience a range of emotion and understanding, and it is quite possible that, for some at least, the experience will be spiritual in nature, some kind of *memento mori*. The important point is that the website is claiming that the primary *intent* of the display is not mere entertainment, but understanding and enlightenment. In this context, however, another event organized by von Hagens seems somewhat strange. This was the autopsy conducted in public in 2002, and the subsequent broadcast of excerpts from it on a widely viewed television channel (albeit late at night). Miah and Rich (2008) have sought to assess how this should be described. Was it entertainment, education or art? Miah and Rich note that the primary justification of this had to be that it was educational, since the aesthetic element clearly present in *Body Worlds* could not be claimed for this event. The educational value would come from dispelling the mystery which usually surrounds such activities and encouraging the viewers to confront their own mortality and perceive the vulnerabilities of their own bodies. Thereby we would be encouraged to escape the denial of physical reality which characterizes our sanitized society and to 'engage with the messiness of being human' (Miah and Rich 2008: 578). However, as Miah and Rich point out, the television programme seemed to stress quite different things, with the cameras scanning the reactions on the faces of the audience rather than engaging the viewer in what was actually taking place. Moreover, the audience seemed to treat the event as a spectacle, not an educational experience. Commenting on the spontaneous applause, which came when von Hagens removed the internal organs, Miah and Rich conclude:

> This somewhat awkward ripple of appreciation seemed to reinforce the performance-like or sensationalistic nature of this event. More likely, however, it was an indication of the audience's unease, provoked by the manner of removal, which resembled the triumph of a child delivery or, indeed, the manner in which a magician removes a rabbit from a hat.
>
> (Miah and Rich 2008: 578)

It would seem, then, that the ambiguity of what von Hagens is really doing remains. Barilan (2006) offers a thought experiment to clarify the issues at stake. Imagine, he says, that the technology advances to the point where we can produce plastic models like those of *Body Worlds*, which are as accurate and artistic and which are no more expensive to produce, but which do *not* require the use of cadavers. Would we be morally indifferent to which method was then used? Barilan thinks not, arguing that plastination becomes immoral if we do not need to utilize cadavers at all. But judging from the language of the *Body Worlds* website, I think von Hagens would disagree. For him, it seems, the fact that this plastic model *was once a living human being* is part of the significance of our reactions to it. I think he would say that it is this individual history (albeit unknown to us in any detail) that adds to our fascination and our enlightenment. We might equally expect that people would not attend in their millions an exhibition that offered only accurate simulacra of dissected dead bodies. They have come to see revealed the mysteries of the dead, and so the moral ambiguity remains.

Gifts of knowledge

We have seen how the ambiguity surrounding the work of Gunther von Hagens relates to his claim to be creating educational and enlightening experiences for the viewers of his exhibitions. When it comes to more orthodox uses of cadavers in post mortem examinations and in anatomical dissection as part of medical training, the issues seem clearer. Such interference with the body of the dead person gives either insight into the causes of death or the development of anatomical knowledge and surgical skills. These are the first of the 'gifts from the dead' that I consider – gifts of knowledge. Yet this area is also not without controversy.

The history of cadaveric dissection is certainly a colourful one (for good surveys of the history, see Richardson 1987; Sawday 1995; Jones 2002). In mediaeval times dissection was carried out in public on executed criminals and its main purpose seems to have been to demonstrate the anatomical descriptions in traditional medical texts – even when the actual structures of the body did not conform to them (Jones 2002: 38)! As we saw earlier, the advent of detailed anatomical examination and research using cadaveric dissection came with the work of Vesalius in the early sixteenth century. In addition Renaissance artists, notably Leonardo da Vinci, dissected corpses and made detailed drawings in order to aid them in the depiction of the human figure. As the importance of anatomical dissection for medical training became more and more recognized, the need for bodies increased, and fresh scandals arose. The 'resurrectionists' of the eighteenth and early nineteenth centuries supplied the demand by digging up newly interred corpses and selling them to surgeon anatomists and medical schools. Since the rich could protect their dead from grave-robbers through locked tombs and other protective devices, the poor became the chief victims of this practice. The culmination of this grisly trade came in the actions of the notorious Burke and Hare in Edinburgh and Bishop and Williams in London, who increased the quota available through the murder of their chosen victims. A notable aspect of all of this history is that dissection of the dead body was seen as a shameful thing, one which stigmatized the dead person and reinforced their marginality in society. Sawday (1995) describes the deliberate intention of the English Murder Act of 1752 to deter criminals by enforcing dissection after execution:

> What was needed, it was felt, was a punishment so draconian, so appalling, that potential criminals would be terrified at the fate which awaited them in the event of their detection. Some new horror was called for which would thwart delinquent desires on the part of the unruly metropolitan populace ... Dissection was to be understood as a specific alternative to the other form of public display encouraged by the authorities – the gibbeting[6] of the corpse after death.
>
> (Sawday 1995: 54)

When this practice was finally abandoned in Britain in the nineteenth century, through the passing of the Anatomy Act of 1831, the need for cadavers for dissection was met instead by confiscating the bodies of paupers, taken from hospitals and workhouses, when there was no one to pay for the funeral. As Richardson comments: 'What had for generations been a feared and hated punishment for murder became one for poverty' (1987: xv).

Clearly, then, the history of anatomical dissection does not merit the description of '*gifts*' from the dead! There had been no act of giving by the dead person. Rather, whether by robbery or murder, punishment for crime, or from the helplessness of destitution and poverty, the bodies on the anatomist's table had been appropriated by society for the advancement of medical science and the training of doctors. The transition from this situation to that of voluntary donation has come about through a series of later Anatomy Acts in various countries, which have enabled a shift in emphasis from abandonment and forcible removal of bodies to premortem altruism by the dead person. However, it is only in relatively recent times (since the 1960s) that bequeathed bodies have become the main source of cadavers in both the UK and the USA (Jones 2002). In other countries unclaimed bodies are still a major source, due to cultural or religious requirements to dispose of the body rapidly, with appropriate ceremony and intact.

Inside the dissection room

However, if a person does decide to gift their body for the training of medical students and doctors, what does the gift accomplish? Entry to the anatomy dissection room[7] has long been seen as a rite of passage for first year medical students. In entering a place where preserved dead bodies are cut up they begin to take on the special role of medical practitioners, to whom privileged access to the bodies of the living and the dead is granted. They may also be challenged to find the right emotional maturity to deal professionally with sights which the ordinary member of the public is likely to find frightening or nauseating. In his intensive study of a group of American medical students experiencing cadaveric dissection for the first time, Hafferty has documented the range of experience and emotion they can go through over the year. Hafferty describes the cadaver as 'ambiguous man', and illustrates the ambiguity with these reflections from one of the students:

> When we uncovered the bodies, everybody was very, very quiet. I just didn't know what to think. They looked real, but then again they didn't ... It didn't look like a person, but rather kind of bizarre, grotesque, disgusting ... but it didn't look like a dead person either, and when you start thinking that, you think, 'What are dead people supposed to look like?' and you start getting all confused.
>
> (Hafferty 1991: 98)

Hafferty found that about 7 per cent of that student group dreaded the experience of entering the dissection room for the first time, but that in the actual situation most of the students found it difficult to adopt a totally detached attitude all of the time. Emotional discomfort levels rose when certain parts of the cadaver were uncovered or were dissected – the hand and arm, the head, the abdomen and the pelvic and perineal regions. Hafferty concludes that this discomfort was caused by 'the rather persistent re-emergence of the cadaver as a human referent' (1991: 110), and he suggests that students who were prepared to use this experience to prevent themselves from becoming overly cold and detached as doctors would have made an important step in the journey towards becoming humane physicians. Other studies (see Jones 2000: 69f.) have confirmed that for about 5 per cent of students the experience can cause at least transient emotional problems. One study (Finkelstein and Mathers 1990) identified severe symptoms of the kind experienced in post-traumatic stress disorder. So is cadaveric dissection really a worthwhile educational method for producing doctors of the future? Fennell and Jones (1992) found that the main motivation of those who donated their bodies to medical schools was to aid in the advancement of medical science and teaching. (Most did not realize that the cadavers are used only for teaching, not for research, though they had been fully informed about this.) Not everyone would agree that anatomical dissection is in fact a necessary component of medical training and a number of medical schools have not included it in their curriculum or have discontinued it. McLachlan *et al.* (2004), in a paper explaining the decision of a new medical school in the UK (the Peninsula Medical School) not to include it, offer a list of suggested advantages and disadvantages, and conclude that, for general medical training, as opposed to the teaching of surgical skills, there is no evidence to show that it is the most effective way to learn anatomy. So far as the other aspects are concerned, such as the development of professional attitudes and the ability to deal with distressing situations, they point to the ambiguity of the dissection room experience. While it may enable some students to develop a sensitive approach to death and dying, it may also help to reinforce a somewhat cold and callous attitude in others.

The debate on the utility of cadaveric dissection will no doubt continue among medical educators,[8] but in the meantime an important gain in the value of the gift can be assured by allowing the use of donated bodies for both teaching anatomy and advancing research. Provided this is made clear at the time of donation, those who wish to assist in the advance of medicine seem very likely to want to enrich the knowledge they can offer beyond the grave.

Post mortem examination

If there is some uncertainty about the advantages of cadaveric dissection, except for specialist training and for research, no such doubt concerns the importance of postmortem examinations. We have already noted that coronial autopsies are a central aspect of crime detection – as well as establishing innocence (for example to distinguish cases of sudden infant death from deliberate injury of the child). Retention of tissue and organs is clearly also necessary here if it is integral to the eventual solution of the crime. (In the retained organs controversy the problem was retention for other unauthorized purposes.) The elective or hospital postmortem is also of huge potential benefit. First, it plays a key role in clinical audit, allowing surgical and medical treatments to be assessed for their effectiveness, as well as checking on the accuracy of the diagnosis and the cause of death (and so what is entered on the death certificate). But in addition it provides information about new, hitherto undiagnosed diseases, about environmental factors in disease causation and about the iatrogenic effects of some treatments. Research on material retained after autopsy is also a major source of medical progress, with stored slides and samples being used many years after the death when new hypotheses arise. Finally, observation of the examination itself and study of the subsequent slides are key aspects of medical training at both general and specialist levels.

There can be little doubt, then, that permission for autopsy is a really valuable gift which a dying person[9] or the surviving relatives can offer to others. Sadly the rate of elective postmortems has dropped dramatically in many countries – by as much as 40–50 per cent in the USA, for example (Jones 2000: 80). This drop does not seem to be related to a reluctance amongst families to agree, despite recent controversies over organ retention. Studies suggest that it is the reluctance of doctors to request it that is the main factor (Jones 2000: 80; Burton and Underwood 2003; Snowdon *et al.* 2004). Here, then, is a gift from the dead which can and should be made, if only the doctors of the future will stop seeing death as always a failure and possibly a threat to their own competence. As we see next, death can also be a source of life.

The gift of life

We saw in Chapter 3 how the dead can maintain the lives of the living through the 'harvesting' of their kidneys for transplantation. But the use of the dead as resources for transplantation medicine is, of course, much more extensive than the use of kidneys for treating chronic renal failure. Lives can be saved by means of transplantation of hearts, lungs and a range of other vital organs from the newly dead, while sight can be restored through the use of corneas from the dead. In most cases the success of the transplantation will depend on both tissue matching and the capacity of the transplant to continue to function after removal from one body and incorporation into another. The viability of the organ will thus depend on whether the body of the person from whom it was removed was still, in some biological sense, alive. Clearly, then, two key issues arise: the definition of death; and the nature of the consent to removal of the organ.

Brain death

It would be widely agreed that death of a living organism is not so much a single event, but rather an irreversible process. Medical technology has made it possible to arrest the process (perhaps indefinitely), through the use of ventilators and heart–lung machines. But when considering the death of a human being we need to resolve the question of whether, even though the body continues to have its functions maintained, the *person* is dead. This question arises, quite apart from the issue of transplantation, since decisions have to be made about the discontinuation of life support when there is no prospect of a return to consciousness and to interpersonal relationships for the affected individual. Considerations of this kind have led to the concept of 'brain death', as the criterion for when the *process* of death is irreversible and efforts to maintain biological life are futile. However, the precise definition of this term has proved to be contentious. The main disagreement is between those who advocate *whole brain death*, which requires that both the higher (cortical) and lower (brainstem) parts of the brain are ceasing to function,[10] and those who advocate *higher brain death* (cessation of function of the cerebral hemispheres, resulting in irreversible loss of consciousness, and the abilities to think, feel and relate to others).

Jones, after surveying the arguments on both sides of this disagreement, concludes:

> the meaningfulness of an individual's existence is open to question once irreversible higher brain death is definitely diagnosed. That individual life is at an end, the irreversibility of the condition eliminating any potential for future relationships, for self-awareness, or for plans of any description. The apparent life of the patient's body should be handled sensitively,

both for relatives and hospital staff, and out of respect for the person he was. The living body of a dead patient represents the remnants of a human life.

(Jones 2000: 224)

Jones is clearly thinking here of situations when the family is approached to consider agreement to the use of the brain dead person as an organ donor. For families, the acceptance of death when the body's systems are kept functioning artificially, and so the body is still warm and breathing, is bound to be difficult, and the decision to agree to switch off the life support systems can be hard.[11] This, then, leads us to the issue of consent for the use of the dead as organ sources.

Consent

In the retained organs controversy discussed earlier, it emerged very clearly that many families would have been glad for the organs of their relative to be retained if they had been asked, and if they had been assured that it was likely to bring benefit to others. Here at least they could see some good coming out of their tragic loss. In one case, parents in fact offered their child's organs:

I could not accept that I had not buried Joseph whole, nor that his organs would have been taken without our consent. What makes their actions even more baffling is that we even offered Joseph's organs for transplant after he died but were told they would not be of any use.

(Bristol Royal Infirmary Inquiry 2000)

Such findings from the various Inquiries led the British government to seek revision of the legislation on the uses of tissue, in order to make the centrality of consent unambiguous. I shall discuss these provisions shortly, but first we should note that not everyone agrees that consent is necessary or appropriate when dead bodies are used for clearly beneficial purposes.

In an issue of the *Journal of Medical Ethics* dealing with organ and tissue donation, H. E. Emson, writing as a forensic pathologist, claims that 'the human body can only legitimately be regarded as on an extended loan from the biomass to the individual' (2003: 125). From this observation Emson concludes that the human cadaver must be viewed merely as a resource for those who may benefit from it, and that it is 'immoral' to require consent for cadaveric donation. (This approach to the body is reminiscent of Frank Herbert's science fiction novel *Dune* (1968), in which a desert people render dead bodies into their constituent elements as soon as death occurs, to augment the vital resource of water.)

In *Wonderwoman and Superman*, John Harris makes the same point as Emson in equally unambiguous terms. Discussing the problem of seeking consent from relatives for the use of cadaveric organs for transplantation, he puts forward the idea that a change in public policy would remove what he sees as the irrational demand that relatives should have a say in what happens to human tissue after death, since this is merely a problem of emotion:

> The solution to the problem of sensibilities is of course to determine that cadavers, like the foreshore, belong to the state and that therefore neither relatives nor the former 'owners' of the cadavers would have any binding interest in their fate. People would, I believe, soon get used to the idea ... and the automatic public ownership of dead bodies and their bodily products would remove the need to interpose intrusive requests between people and their grief.
>
> (Harris 1992: 102)

We can see here the rationalist dismissal of emotion at its strongest. Even if it were theoretically justified, the idea that human societies are likely to 'get used to the idea' that the state takes charge of their dead is in flat contradiction to human responses to the disposal of dead bodies, from the earliest evidence of human communities. Respectful treatment of the dead is what has been described as a 'human universal' (Brown 1991: 139). In any case, the argument that the dead and the families of the dead have no interests in the dead body seems simplistic. As Brazier points out, the cost to families in terms of offence to their religious values and emotional health can be considerable (2002: 565). For the deceased person also both harm and benefit can come to their reputation and to the way they are remembered after death through the treatment of their dead body – why else is it still, even today, the practice in some brutal conflicts to desecrate the bodies of hated enemies? (The dilemma of *Antigone* lives on.)

However, the force of the argument put forward by Emson and Harris comes from a comparison of the scale of benefits and harms which can come to the affected parties through the failure to realize the full potential of cadaveric organs and cadaveric tissue for medical research and therapy. Here is where a mediating position can be suggested between state expropriation of the body and an insistence on active donation *premortem*. This mediating position is sometimes described as 'presumed consent', or alternatively as the 'opt out' as opposed to the 'opt in' position. With such a policy, the person's organs can be used unless he or she has specifically declared that this should not happen. The presumption here is that most people will be happy for their body to be used for such good ends, and that people who find it objectionable, on religious or other grounds, will ensure they make their objection known. (There are variations on this system, for example giving specific opportunities to register an objection when enrolling in a medical clinic or applying for a driver's licence.)

At the other end of this spectrum of approaches to consent are forms of legislation that make removal of organs or tissue *postmortem* a criminal offence in the absence of 'appropriate consent' by either the donor or the family. The Human Tissue Act 2004, enacted in England, Wales and Northern Ireland as a response to the controversy over organ retention, provides an example of this third position. Here consent is central to virtually all uses of tissue and organs from the deceased; however, there is then a hierarchy of authorized consent. At the top of the hierarchy is the consent of the person prior to death. If this has been given, or if a clear refusal of consent has been made, then this cannot be countermanded. Next on the hierarchy is any person nominated by the deceased to give or withhold consent on his behalf. Again, this cannot be countermanded. Finally, in the absence of either of these forms of consent or refusal, a list of persons qualified to give consent is given, and an order of priority is defined according to their relationship to the deceased.

Which of these three positions best meets the competing requirements of the deceased person, the family and the beneficiaries of the donations? It is relevant to note that the very successful cadaveric donation schemes in some European countries (see Chapter 3) are all forms of the opt out or presumed consent position, but that in most of them organs would *not* be removed against the wishes of the family. In countries where the family has no say (for example Austria) retrieval rates are no better (Healy 2006). This suggests that, even from a pragmatic point of view, insisting on the removal of the organs against family opposition is unlikely to produce the desired outcome overall. It may even result in more people opting out, in order to save any distress to their own families in the future. Equally, it seems bound to create a climate of suspicion and mistrust between the medical profession and the general public, rather than fostering a climate of partnership in what is obviously a worthwhile endeavour.

Ideally, then, we should be holding on to the concept of gift when considering how life can come from death. After death, a person's body can be of very small consequence to him or her, unless the treatment of it would offend dearly held beliefs or values. But it is of great consequence to the grieving family. We need not suppose that the dead body is the *property* of the family in order to regard them as deeply involved in the question of donation. Gifts *from* the dead are not necessarily gifts *by* the dead. It is best to see the family either as honouring the dead person's wishes by consenting to their expressed wish to be a donor or, when this wish is not known, as honouring the memory of the dead person through the hope of continued life for someone else and their family. The worst scenario would be one in which the state requisitions the dead to serve the common good. The conscription of the dead might save some lives – though the evidence is missing for such a claim – but only in the narrowest sense would it enhance our life together. As before it is the *gift* of the body which unites us, not its expropriation.

Gifts of memory

An integrative theme of this chapter has been that death and life are inter-twined. This is so in two senses: first, that part of the meaning of human life is that we know it must end in death; and, second, that from death new life springs – we can receive gifts from the dead that maintain and enhance our lives. But this could be an overly romantic, not to say mawkishly sentimental, view of death. Certainly we are capable of accepting our finitude, even of welcoming it as some kind of culmination and fulfilment of our time on earth. Rabinranath Tagore captures this sense of tranquillity in his poem 'Last Curtain':

> I know that the day will come
> when my sight of this earth shall be lost,
> and life will take its leave in silence,
> drawing the last curtain over my eyes.
> Yet stars will watch at night,
> and morning rise as before,
> and hours heave like sea waves casting up pleasures and pains ...
> Things that I longed for in vain
> and things that I got
> – let them pass.
> Let me but truly possess
> the things that I ever spurned
> and overlooked.
>
> (Tagore 1914)

Yet in tension with such acceptance is a sense of injustice and anger that our lives and the lives of those we love must end. As Dylan Thomas pleaded with his father to do, we too may 'rage against the dying of the light' (from the poem 'Do Not Go Gentle into That Good Night' (Thomas 1971)). And it is not just people that we grieve to lose – the earth itself is hard to relinquish. As Kazantzakis says in *Report to Greco*:

> A man can tell himself he is satisfied and peaceful; he can say he has no more wants, that he has fulfilled his duty and is ready to leave. But the heart resists, clutching the stones and the grass, it implores, 'Stay a little!'
>
> (Kazantzakis 1965: 18)

Of course, the reality is that we have to let go, and that people have to let go of us. To this extent Emson is obviously right – our bodies are 'on an extended loan from the biomass' (2003: 125) – or, in the more poetic language of the Bible, 'dust thou art and unto dust shalt thou return' (*Genesis* 3:19). We may seek a permanent habitation on earth, but the crumbling and illegible tombstones of bygone ages and the raided tombs of the kings of ancient Egypt bear ample testimony to the folly of such dreams. All that we can leave, in the final analysis, are memories, treasured by those who survive us. These are precious gifts indeed, as any bereaved person will testify, but, of course, the time will come when we shall not even be a memory in the minds of the living.

Why, then, speak of 'gifts of memory' from the dead? Isn't this just one more illusion to ease the pain of life's fragility and transitoriness?[12] I believe we can gain insights here from what are often regarded as 'primitive" ideas of the homecoming of dead bodies. In recent years, with the increasing self-awareness and activism of indigenous peoples throughout the world, there has been a major move towards the repatriation of human remains held in Western museums but sourced from all over the world. The Natural History Museum in London provides a case in point. The Museum holds the national collection of human remains in the UK, comprising 19,950 specimens (varying from a complete skeleton to a single finger bone). The remains represent a worldwide distribution of the human population and a timescale of 500,000 years. The majority of the collection (54 per cent) represents individuals from the UK. The Natural History Museum's Human Remains Advisory Panel was set up in 2006. The remit of the panel is to provide independent advice to the Trustees of the museum on claims for return of human remains to countries of origin. Acting on the advice of this panel in 2007, the Trustees decided to transfer the remains of seventeen Tasmanian aboriginal people to the Australian Government, which has designated the Tasmanian Aboriginal Centre to be the receivers of the Tasmanian remains. The Trustees also decided to return the skull of an aboriginal person from Australia to the Australian Government. However, the museum also retained the right to carry out further observations and tests on the remains prior to transfer. As a result, the decision can be seen as an attempt at a compromise between the demands of the two parties in contention – their own scientists, who wanted to use the remains for their research, and the Aboriginal people, who wished to give their ancestors due respect and a proper resting place.

Jones has explored in detail the character of the worldwide debate about the repatriation of human remains, which has taken place in many countries, including the USA, Canada, South Africa, Australia and New Zealand. I shall not enter into the details of this debate in this chapter, since for our purposes the important feature of it is the different view of time (and so of history) held by indigenous peoples and Western scientists. For scientific researchers the remains are an important aid in dating human history. Theirs is a linear view of time, whereas for indigenous peoples time is better described as circular – the past comes round to meet us. Jones uses the Maori understanding of the past as being *in front of, not behind* the individual because of the presence of the ancestors to explain why ancient human remains are so important to them:

the Maori regard the past as intertwined with the present, and feel a spiritual link with their ancestors, who are accorded much higher value than in those cultures where they merely signify part of an historical record. Hence demonstration of respect for indigenous people's cultural beliefs must also incorporate respect for the remains of their ancestors.

(Jones 2000: 130)

This helps us to understand why the storing of ancestral bones in a Western museum or the display there of the skulls of people long dead causes such distress to their descendants. For them, there is a place to which such remains rightly belong, and this has to be in the land of their people. (The need to be buried in the right place, with one's people, remains a central issue for New Zealand Maori to this day.)

But these cultural differences are not just curiosities, and not only important for us in ensuring cultural sensitivity. They carry important messages for our own cultures. Many people in the West today seem to be in a desperate search to find their roots. Business is booming for websites advertising genealogical record searches or tracing of ancestry though DNA analysis (see, for example, the website of Genelex Corporation, www.healthanddna.com). It seems that people in post-industrial societies need to know where they have come from and where they belong, just as people we may call 'primitive' do. This begins to make sense when we realize how, in the frenetic development of the post-industrial world, we have lost all sense of distinctive location in time and space. Now we live in cyberspace, with instant communication making distance and diversity a thing of the past. Moreover, as we saw in Chapter 5, our post-modern world makes all of 'reality' into simulacra, into whatever images we choose to take as normative. So we can find ourselves adrift in a world which we can never call our own, since there need be no permanence, no enduring values, nothing that ultimately matters to us. Losing our embodiment in a particular time and place, we lose any sense of our uniqueness – we lose our identity.

That is why the gift of memories which the dead offer us is so fundamentally necessary to us, whether we come from the East or West, North or South, and whatever our particular ancestry. The offence of the well-meaning palaeontologist who dates the bones of our forbears is that, in common with so much in our age, the information extracted tells us nothing of real use to us, nothing about how our past may help us now, nothing about how it may live on in us in a positive way. Instead, our being as individual persons is reduced to a string of numbers, rather like the identity card codes by which many modern societies track their citizens.

The gift of memory can take us back to a physical place of our ancestors – a place transformed no doubt by all the rapid change of our era, so not the place they knew – yet still a place where we can reconnect to earth and, for a time, leave cyberspace. This may seem somewhat mystical, but in fact it relates wholly to the *corporeal*, to the embodiment of persons and their physical location on earth. For those millions of us who no longer know ourselves as a people of the land – what the Maori call *tangata phenua* – this is a major challenge. But one thing is clear. We need to be rooted again in the earth, to which we shall all return – and here, perhaps, the dead can help us with their gifts of memory. But also, as we shall see in the final chapter (Chapter 7), even this last resting place is under threat.

Chapter 7

Together at last

A constant theme throughout this book has been the disjunction that can occur between ourselves as conscious, planning, calculating, reasoning, dreaming, speculating, imagining and emotionally complex beings, and ourselves as sensate organisms located in a physical environment and seeking survival through constant adaptation within it, finite beings who grow and die and inevitably merge once more with the organic mix from which we emerged. We can speak of this disjunction as mind versus body, spirit versus flesh, conscious being versus embodied being – even reason versus emotion, if emotion is (wrongly)[1] understood purely as a physiological reaction related to survival. But as soon as we make these oppositions we must surely be aware that there is something fundamentally wrong with them. No doubt they seem neat and tidy enough, perhaps quite reassuring if we find emotion in ourselves and others somewhat disturbing and unpredictable, or if we prefer the seeming boundlessness of thought to the limitations and frustrations of being in a body. No doubt, too, the inescapable awareness of our own death and the death of those we love makes us seek things of enduring value – 'the eternal now', as theologian Paul Tillich (1963) put it. There are many paths to temporary transcendence of the limitations of the body, provided by religion, music, art, contemplation of nature, or the intimacy and ecstasy of personal relationships. But, despite the delights of intellectual speculation, the bracing challenges of seeking clarity of thought and of achieving fair and reasoned debate with others, despite the joy of being 'taken out of ourselves' through love, the creative arts or the awesome beauty of the natural world, we remain what we inevitably are – vulnerable living tissue, located in time and space. Our bodies and the bodies of our fellow humans are always with us, an inescapable concomitant of being living, conscious beings. If we ignore this aspect of human life, we will end up with an abstract, theoretical and ultimately irrelevant bioethics.

In the previous chapters, I have tried to offer a perspective on some of the bioethical debates of our time that will help us to gain a richer understanding of how the human body can retain its moral value in the biomedical sphere, rather than becoming demoted to just another material resource, ripe for exploitation by our burgeoning medical and biotechnological indus-tries. This may seem a somewhat ambitious project, but in fact it is quite modest. I have not tried to formulate a new kind of ethical theory, for example something like 'Embodied Ethics' (see Weiss 1999: Ch. 7). Indeed, I have offered no specific solutions to quite a few of the medical ethics dilem-mas of our day, such as whether surgeons should cut off healthy limbs, whether anorexics should be force-fed or whether cosmetic medicine can be seen as an appropriate activity for the medical profession. Such issues must be resolved, of course, just as we have to resolve questions like whether the trade in body parts should be legalized, whether donors of tissue should share in subsequent commercial gains, whether dead bodies should be pub-licly displayed or whether relatives should have a veto on cadaveric trans-plantation. My position on some of these questions has already been implicit or explicit in the previous chapters. My aim, however, has not been to pro-vide set and final answers to these contemporary debates. Rather, I have seen myself as an advocate for our neglected and frequently despised partner, the body, in the hope that our decisions on these specific issues will be more considered and reflective. We can defend positions either in terms of our duties to self and others or in terms of the consequences of our actions for human welfare, but in either case we need to know what value the human body carries in such calculations of moral weight. Here the problem is that we fail to see the full reality of our own bodies and the bodies of others, even though we may seem to be quite obsessed with them. It is as though we have lost contact for years with our closest friend, and in this time we hold on to some idealized image of him or her as a kind of consolation for our loss. But what we need is to be re-united, to be 'together at last' and rediscover the true value of the friendship. This is the metaphor that underlies my con-cluding comments in this book, as I consider three aspects of such a re-union: re-union with ourselves; re-union with others; and re-union with the material world we inhabit.

Re-uniting the self

We have seen in the previous pages the many powerful ways in which people can be alienated from their own bodies. For some, like the transsexual and (perhaps) the sufferer from BIID, there may be a solution through a physical alteration of the body they were born with, but for others the alienation resists a cure. Most tragically, those who despise their body shape may destroy their health and indeed life itself in their attempts to find a body they can live with. Equally tragic are those situations where *others* decide that one's body is wrong – children whose parents impose surgery in the name of welfare, or people whose bodily differences are made into physical and social handicaps by the insensitivity and indifference of the society in which they live. But these extreme examples are simply one end of a spectrum of bodily dystopias in which we all (potentially) have a place. Carl Elliott neatly sums up what he calls the 'tyranny of happiness' and its effect on the way we treat our bodies in our consumer orientated society:

> Some people want their legs lengthened, while others want them amputated. Black folks rub themselves with cream to make their skin lighter, while white folks broil in tanning parlors to make their skin darker. Bashful men get ETS surgery to reduce blood flow above the neck, while elderly men take Viagra to increase blood flow below the belt.
>
> (Elliott 2003: 198)

Elliott explains these curious ways in which we try to overcome our body 'failures' (the embarrassing relation who will let us down in company!) in terms of the notion of our lives as a project which *we* have to manage properly. The aim of the project is to find fulfilment, to be truly happy, to be genuinely oneself. The trouble is nobody can tell anyone else how this quest is to be successful. All I can tell is the feeling of discontent with my life – 'Life is a short sweet ride, and I am spending it all in the station' (Elliott 2003: 300). So all the new technologies of enhancement seductively beckon me: they offer me the nirvana of 'the real me' emerging once the changes are made to my troublesome body. In reality, of course, all they offer is a carefully crafted image. As Elliott observes, 'Authenticity can be packaged, commodified and put to work for capitalism' (2003: 128). However, the image-makers cannot remove our inner discontent.

To be sure, there can be no simple answer to such civil war within the self – and Elliott, to his credit, certainly does not offer one. But one could make a start by celebrating both diversity and change in the human body. Perhaps at no time in human history has there been the possibility of us seeing with our own eyes the richness of our human heritage and so of recognizing that there is no normative human body. (We are well beyond the cold symmetry of classical Greek sculpture.) A walk down the streets of some of the world's great cities – London, New York, Singapore – reveals a kaleidoscope of bone structures, eye shapes and colours, body shape and posture, hair texture, skin colour, adornment of the body, and so on. Further diversity is added by a willingness to play with hair styles, body piercing, tattooing and the ambiguous symbols of gender.

Of course, some of this range of bodily appearance has been culturally determined and, in the modern era, is the product of changing fashion. Moreover, our physical diversity can function merely as a stimulus to discrimination and prejudice. Not everyone is willing to accept difference, and many people are threatened by it. Nevertheless, in our age, as never before, there seems to be some hope for the *celebration* of difference, rather than the fear of it. And if this is so, then perhaps we can also see that conforming to fashion need be no more than human playfulness, a game in which there are no losers, except those unfortunate enough to believe that fashion proves their value as persons. We may make changes to our bodily appearance without supposing that these determine our social or personal worth. If we reject the confusion of personal worth with personal appearance, then we can get to know our body in a new way, allowing it to change and age, accepting a lessening of powers as part of the natural rhythm of organic life, experimenting with different ways of appearing. In this way we restore the friendship with our body. It is, after all, our lifelong companion, uniquely ours.

In his trenchant and entertaining critique of post-modern philosophy, *The Illusions of Postmodernism*, Terry Eagleton has persuasively mapped out the relationship between nature and culture in human life:

> It is important to see, as postmodernism largely does not, that we are not 'cultural' rather than 'natural' creatures, but cultural beings by virtue of our nature, which is to say by virtue of the sorts of bodies we have and the kind of world to which they belong. Because we are all born prematurely, unable to look after ourselves, our nature contains a yawning abyss into which culture must move otherwise we would quickly die. And this move into culture is at once our splendour and our catastrophe ... The linguistic animal has the edge over its fellow creatures in all kinds of ways: it can be sardonic or play the trombone, torture children and stockpile nuclear weapons.
>
> (Eagleton 1996: 73)

Eagleton goes on to point out that 'Slugs and beavers cannot lunge at each other with knives, unless they are doing it on the quiet, but neither can they practise surgery' (1996: 73). He might have added, nor do they worry about ageing or write poems about death. It is this interplay between our 'natural' selves and our 'cultural' selves – continuing throughout our lives – that creates the moral ambiguity of the way we treat our bodies and the bodies of others. We can reflect upon our bodies, valuing or disvaluing them. We can alter them in all sorts of ways – but we literally cannot live without them.

The lives of others

I have taken the title of this section from the Academy Award winning movie *The Lives of Others* (2006), written and directed by Florian Henckel von Donnersmarck. The film is set in East Germany shortly before *Perestroika* and the fall of the Berlin Wall. It centres round three main characters, a playwright, an actress, who is his girlfriend, and a Stasi agent, who is assigned to carry out a twenty-four hour surveillance of them, through microphones concealed in every room of their apartment. The film is a remarkable portrayal of the transformation of the agent as he increasingly enters into the world of those he is secretly observing. In a quite profound way he enters into 'the lives of others', and this transposes his whole value system from its previous ideological stance to sympathy for their criticism of the Communist regime.

It is possible for any of us to enter into the lives of other human beings, though perhaps not in this radical and transformative way. We cannot enter the lives of slugs and beavers, whales and dolphins – even of the animals we domesticate, like dogs, cats and budgerigars – in such a way, though we may sense some of what they experience from knowledge of their behaviour. Our most vital link with our fellow human beings is created by the fact that they have bodies like ours. So, although we cannot literally think their thoughts or experience their feelings, we can easily recognize and respond to them, sensing their pain and distress, or their feelings of joy, fear or boredom, almost as though they were our own. Of course, we also have the advantage of sharing with them the capacity for language, and this allows us to check out our responses directly with them. Thanks to language, we can also respond to and empathize with the thoughts and feelings of people we have never met, through the written and spoken word. However, this mediated response is possible only because they share our world of bodily experience. (Or at least we think they do – we might of course be duped by a computer generated novel or poem!)

It is on this basis that it is justifiable (and not 'speciesist' in a prejudiced sense) to give special moral value to human bodies and bodily material, and so to oppose their commodification, their demotion to mere organic stuff of marketable value. This is not to say that we give *absolute* moral value to such material, to suppose that the objectification of (say) a human kidney is tantamount to treating a person as though she were merely an item for sale. However, the risk of this slide to the disrespect of persons is present as soon as we begin to disaggregate the organic unity on which human life depends. For this reason I have suggested earlier (Chapters 2 and 4) that we use the somewhat vague term 'respect' for our approach to human material and that we need to exempt it from the simple equivalences of the market. In the case of material far removed from its origin in the body of the donor and clearly within a market setting already (the 'tissue economy' problem), I have supported the idea of the creation of a 'biocommons'. In these ways, we are seeking to recognize the 'leaky' boundaries of our shared bodily life. Rather than seeing ourselves as isolated self-interested negotiators seeking maximum advantage for ourselves, we share in our communal destiny, as creatures with a common origin and a common fate. We enter the lives of others.

So far I have been discussing the re-uniting of our lives with those of our fellow humans at the somewhat abstract level of the donation of body parts and body tissue. At the more obvious level of whole body interaction, it is still easy to overlook the significance of the body. Here, of course, we get into many psychological and social complexities. There are huge cultural differences in such things as appropriate touching, maintaining bodily space, covering or revealing parts of the body (from the bikini to the burkha), to say nothing of the variations in cultural norms for social and physical relationships between and within the sexes. However, while recognizing these complexities, we need to avoid the over-rationalization of the way we can care for each other. In *Body Images: Embodiment as Intercorporeality*, Gail Weiss (1999) explores the reflections of Simone de Beauvoir on her dying mother's refusal to accept her own imminent death. For Beauvoir, a lover and a philosophical follower of Sartre, such self-deception would normally be morally unacceptable – 'bad faith', in Sartre's term. Yet her mother was resolute in maintaining that she was not dying and sought from Simone and her sister confirmation of that protective self-deception. Weiss argues that this presented Simone with a conflict between her intellectual conviction and her visceral reaction to her mother's attempts to cope with her fate. She chose to take part in the deception, because that is what her mother's 'living corpse' demanded of her:

> The transition from my mother to a living corpse had been definitively established. The world had shrunk to the size of her room: when I crossed Paris in a taxi I saw nothing more than a stage with extras walking about on it. My real life took place at her side, and it had only one aim – protecting her.
>
> (Beauvoir 1965: 73, cited in Weiss 1999: 150)

Weiss comments about this passage that 'Beauvoir herself is compelled to grant the moral legitimacy of these bodily imperatives, despite the fact that her mother's interests, needs and desires are so very much in conflict with her own' (1999: 150). Whether or not one shares Weiss's concept of 'bodily imperatives', the main point she is making is a central one for understanding the lives of others in a bodily sense. The sheer nature of our presence with the other person can create interaction which is either therapeutic or disabling.[2] In our body posture, our way of looking, our closeness or distance, the way we touch the other, the timbre of our speech, we create confidence or take away hope. Our bodies interact for good or ill. We can enter into the lives of others in an intellectual way – and this can be helpful and supportive – but more powerful than that is our physical presence. It is no accident that, in medical practice, the most effective medicine can be the doctor herself.

Earthbound

Finally, our body constantly reminds us of our highly ambiguous relationship with the natural world, of which we are inevitably a part. This relationship, as Eagleton put it, is one of both 'splendour and catastrophe'. In a manner and scale quite unlike the influence of any other living creatures, humans have made, and will continue to make, massive changes to the environment on which they depend for their survival. Sigmund Freud wrote of humans having a 'death wish', which he described an 'the urge to return to the quiescence of inorganic matter' (1961: 76). If we have such a wish, it looks close to being fulfilled in the foreseeable future, as our collective efforts to exploit natural resources increasingly threaten the very system upon which life depends. No account of bioethics can possibly be adequate if it ignores this aspect of our bodily existence. We are 'earthbound' in two inter-related senses: we depend utterly upon the earth itself for the continuity of all organic life, including the life of humans; and our last resting place is the earth, that place from which we evolved, as in death our body returns to its constituent elements.

Of course, we can speculate about ways of evading these restrictions on human life as we currently know it. We can shoot our ashes into outer space, if this seems preferable to having them returned to the earth we know; we can hope to colonize other planets or to launch lifeboats into space to escape the earth's demise; we can try to defeat ageing, in the fond hope that there will be an environment to support an ageless and expanding population. No one can say with certainty that none of these things will happen, given the extraordinary ingenuity of human adaptation up to now. But such speculation, while no doubt diverting, is surely also morally irresponsible – it is fiddling while Rome burns! What we need now is the wisdom and humility to know that we are earthbound. We need to know that we depend utterly, and within a very few years, on enough of our fellow humans recognizing that our capacities for calculation, planning and organization, those disembodied parts of ourselves which give us such power, far from enhancing and protecting our bodies, seem bent on their destruction.

So the ultimate issue for ensuring respect for the body in bioethics is not the resolution of our inner disunity or the celebration of a common humanity within our rich diversity, important though these clearly are. It is the restoration of the sustaining relationship between our bodies and the (massively re-engineered) natural world. Here we see the worst consequences of our disregard, if not contempt, for our bodily existence. This is where we have to be determined to be able to say – in the very near future – 'together at last'. Without this final re-union there will be literally no place for human consciousness to be, and our disregard for the body in favour of the glories of the human mind will surely have its day of reckoning.

Notes

1 Why the body matters

1 An early example of this can be found in Kuhse and Singer's discussion of prolonging the lives of handicapped infants, in which they argue that there is no reason to prioritize a severely handicapped human life over the lives of our near cousins in the animal kingdom (see Ch. 6 of Kuhse and Singer 1985).
2 This critique derives from extensive feminist writings on the nature of knowledge, science and theory (Hartsock 1983; Lloyd 1986; Longino 1990, 2002; Harding 2006).
3 These arguments are more fully explored in Chapter 3.
4 In Plato's *Republic* (Book 7), human life is depicted in the memorable image of prisoners chained in a cave and facing a blank wall. Far back in the cave a fire casts shadows onto the wall and between the fire and prisoners people 'carrying all sorts of artifacts, which project above the wall, and statues of men and other animals wrought from stone, wood, and every kind of material; as is to be expected, some of the carriers utter sound while others are silent'. On the basis of this inadequate knowledge, the prisoners draw conclusions about the true nature of the world. In this powerful image, Plato dismisses the body and its sense-experiences as sources of knowledge.
5 This dictum by Kant has been commonly paraphrased as 'Thoughts without content are empty; intuitions without concepts are blind'.

2 My body: property, commodity or gift?

1 The artist Anthony Noel Kelly was convicted of theft in a British court for removing body parts from the anatomy museum of the Royal College of Surgeons and making casts out of them for an art exhibit. The judge decided that the specimens were the property of the College because of the skilled work carried out on them by a previous generation of surgeons. Kelly was sentenced to nine months in prison.
2 In his *Second Treatise on the Government* (1690), Locke wrote:

> Though the earth ... be common to all men, yet every man has a property in his own person: this no body has any right to but himself. The labour of his body, and the work of his hands, we may say, are properly his. Whatsoever then he removes out of the state that nature hath provided, and left it in, he hath mixed his labour with, and joined to it something that is his own, and thereby makes it his property. It being by him removed from the common

state nature hath placed it in, it hath by this labour something annexed to it, that excludes the common right of other men.

(Locke 1986: Ch. 5, Sec. 27)

3 Bentham famously proclaimed that any doctrine of natural rights is 'simple nonsense: natural and imprescriptible rights, rhetorical nonsense – nonsense upon stilts' (see Waldron 1987: 53).
4 See, for example, the United Nations Universal Declaration of Human Rights (UN 1948).
5 This case is more fully discussed in Chapter 4.

3 Body futures

1 See the paper by Radcliffe-Richards *et al.* in *The Lancet*, in which prohibition of the market in body parts is likened to 'ending slum dwelling by bulldozing slums' (Radcliffe-Richards *et al.* 1998: 1951).
2 The 'Blood Compact' (*Pacto de Sangre*) between the Spanish conquistador Legaspi and the Filipino native Sikatuna in 1565 symbolized their friendship against a backdrop of local opposition to foreign incursions into Philippine territory. Legaspi and Sikatuna cut their arms to draw blood that was allowed to flow into a cup. They then drank from the cup to mark the end of their enmity. Citing unnamed Filipino and Spanish historians, Paul Kramer writes: 'it was ancient Philippine custom to seal treaties of alliance or friendship by mixing the blood of leaders' (2006: 59).
3 For further discussion of the impact of HIV contamination of blood, see Weinberg *et al.* 2002; Berridge 1997.
4 Some economists argue that profit should be a solid incentive for commercial blood banks to ensure the safety of their products since publicity concerning unsafe practices could easily drive clients away. Their view is that the government's responsibility should be to ensure that safety guidelines are observed and promptly updated in light of new knowledge. However, experiences with commercial banks in several countries suggest that these safeguards may be insufficient.
5 An example of the problem faced by governments comes from the Philippines, which has outlawed commercial blood banks since 1995, but the association of commercial blood banks was able to get a restraining order from the courts (see *Malaya*, 20 March 2006: 1).
6 Simpson (2004) provides an interesting cultural perspective on a Buddhist view of giving and charity, relating to strategies to encourage the donation of human tissue in Sri Lanka. He notes that traditional understandings of religious duties have been used effectively to enhance donation rates. However he also notes that increasing commercialization is beginning to undercut these traditional values.
7 However, Bob Veatch's essay does read more like an ironic attack on the greed of corporate America than a serious defence of organ sales as a rescue for the poor.
8 One comparator which de Castro does not explore is the common practice in many countries of giving tax exemption for charitable giving. Here is perhaps the best example of how a charitable act would also have a financial reward, in terms of less tax to be paid. This hardly applies directly to the poor people who wish to sell their kidneys, but it does raise in an interesting way the question of whether such charitable donations can genuinely be described as altruistic. The question is raised even more sharply in the case of companies writing off some tax liability this way.
9 My colleague Leonardo de Castro, who has written extensively on the subject of schemes of compensation for donors (2003), has countered this judgment by

commenting in his feedback on the manuscript of this chapter that 'my personal view is that "giving of myself to the other" and "treating my body (note the word 'merely' is absent here) as means to income" are not mutually exclusive. And while it may be demeaning (but not necessarily in a bad way) for a poor person to accept money in return for a kidney so that he could pay for the medical treatment of a sick son or daughter, the act could at the same time be heroic. (Admittedly, this is not the type of situation one is likely to encounter on the ground, with most organ donors being misinformed and ill-advised.)'

10 In August 2008, the world's first ever transplantation of entire arms was performed in Germany (Klinkum rechts der Isar Munich 2008).

11 In May 2005, poverty forced a woman in Bangladesh to place an advertisement in a newspaper offering to sell one of her eyes, though any sale was circumvented by the government, which provided her financial assistance (Waliur 2005).

4 The tissue trove

1 For example the Canavan disease judgment, in which the court found that researchers could not profit from developments of research in which patients and their families had been actively involved beyond the scope of the original consent they had obtained for gaining the samples. The court did not grant a property right to the donors or their families, but rather based the judgment on 'unjust enrichment' (Greenberg v. Miami Children's Hospital Research Institute, Inc. 2003).

2 We may note that organs do not really fit this definition, unless one believes that there is no risk at all to the donor from transplantation.

5 The branded body

1 The full clinical terms for both disorders have 'nervosa' added to the title, but I shall use the shortened terms 'anorexia' and 'bulimia', as these are the ones in popular use.

2 Although the term 'aesthetic' is becoming preferred by practitioners – for example, the main US professional association is called the American Society of Aesthetic Medicine and Surgery and similar titles have been adopted in other countries – I shall use the term 'cosmetic', because it conveys what is intended more accurately than the grandiose term 'aesthetic', which hints at some objective standard of beauty (an issue I shall discuss later in the chapter). See *Oxford English Dictionary* (2005): cosmetic = 'serving to improve the appearance of the body', from the Greek *kosmein*, to arrange or adorn. I shall also use the term 'cosmetic medicine' in places, as well as 'cosmetic surgery', since some procedures for enhancement, such as Botox injections and liposuction, use non-surgical methods.

3 Estimates vary, but increases of at least 200 per cent over less than ten years in common surgical enhancement operations (breast enlargement, face lifts and nose reconstruction) seem well documented (Kuczynski 2006).

4 This is not a view of the beauty of flowers shared by Georges Bataille, one of the advocates of the artistic 'avant-garde' of the early twentieth century. In 'The Language of the Flower' (1929) he wrote: 'even though it gave you the impression of slipping away in a rush of angelic, lyrical purity, the flower seems to brusquely return to its primitive filth ... because flowers don't age honestly like leaves, which lose none of their beauty even after they are dead; flowers wither like simpering, overly made-up old women, dying ridiculously on the same stem that seemed to be bearing them up to the stars' (Bataille 1985). Such an attack on conventional notions of beauty was a feature of the revolt represented by several movements in the early part of the century (see Eco 2007: Chs XIII and XIV).

6 Gifts from the dead

1 The Astronomer Royal, Martin Rees, has a memorable quotation from Woody Allen on this topic: 'Eternity is very long, especially towards the end' (quoted in Rees 1999: 80). I'm indebted to my friend Don Hill for pointing out this quip by Allen.

2 It should be noted that I was a member and the Vice-Chair of the Retained Organs Commission. A more detailed account of the controversy can be found in an article written by me and by a parent whose child's heart was removed, and who was also a member of the Commission (Campbell and Willis 2005).

3 These considerations do not apply to the wholesale harvesting of organs and body parts by one particular pathologist working for Alder Hey children's hospital (see Royal Liverpool Children's Inquiry 2001). However, his actions were clearly not typical of normal pathological practice, when retentions would relate to specific issues, such as cause of death.

4 As we shall see later in the chapter, medical students find these parts of the cadaver the most difficult to deal with also, since they evoke the humanity of the dead person.

5 I have visited the Capuchin Monastery catacombs near Palermo, Sicily, whose dry atmosphere has assisted in the preservation of dead bodies. There are several aisles in the catacombs, ordered according to the occupants – men, women, children, professionals and priests. A particularly striking body is that of a young girl, Rosalia Lombardo, who died in 1920, but still has curly fair hair and a face which looks as though she were asleep. (The method of preserving her is not known now and most of the other bodies, although fully clothed, show signs of emaciation and decay. The practice of placing bodies in the catacomb began in 1599, but is now discontinued. Any member of the public can visit the display upon payment of a small fee.)

6 Gibbeting consisted of hanging the body in chains on a scaffold.

7 This is the term I shall use, though it is notable that some medical schools still use the term 'anatomy theatre', even though there are no viewing galleries as there were in the past in ancient schools like Padua. In the USA, the term 'anatomy lab' (or laboratory) is most commonly used, communicating the scientific purpose of discovery through dissection.

8 It reminds me of the debate about theological education, when I was studying theology in the late 1950s, about whether the ability to read the biblical texts in the original languages was essential for a proper training of the clergy. Many cohorts of students have since graduated with no knowledge of Greek or Hebrew, but I do not know if anyone has assessed the effect on their ministry or the quality of their sermons!

9 My daughter, Isla, who died from cancer when she was still in her thirties, made it very clear that she wanted a postmortem performed, partly so that the effectiveness of the alternative treatment she had used could be assessed and more generally in the hope of helping to prevent others suffering from such a premature death.

10 The death of the brainstem is often accepted as equivalent to whole brain death, since once it ceases to function whole brain death inevitably follows.

11 This is one of the problems in 'opt out' systems, as I discuss when considering consent. In Singapore, where such a system operates, a family became violent when told by the hospital staff that life support was to be removed, claiming their relative should be given a chance to recover, since he did not seem dead to them.

12 Philip Larkin writes bitterly of religion as 'that vast, moth-eaten, musical brocade, created to pretend we never die' (from the poem *Aubade*, in Larkin 1988).

7 Together at last

1 As we saw in Chapter 1, Damasio (1999) makes the point strongly that human emotion has a cognitive and evaluative element, and is rarely merely a simple instinctive response. See also my book *The Gospel of Anger* (Campbell 1986).

2 Beauvoir's description of the shrinking room is powerfully reminiscent of Elaine's Scarry's description of the effects of torture in *The Body in Pain* (1987: 35). In extreme situations of pain the room seems to close in on one, until there is no space for the body at all except that space where pain is everything. Here of course the presence of another person – the torturer – adds to the horror.

Bibliography

American Psychiatric Association (1996) *Diagnostic and Statistical Manual of Mental Disorders*, 4th edn, Washington, DC: American Psychiatric Publishing.

Anderson, E. (1993) *Value in Ethics and Economics*, Cambridge, MA: Harvard University Press.

Andrews, L. B. (1986) 'My body, my property', *Hastings Center Report*, 16 (5): 28–38.

Andrews, L. B. and Nelkin, D. (2001) *Body Bazaar: The Market for Human Tissue in the Biotechnology Age*, New York: Crown Publishers.

Annas, G. J. (1984) 'Life, liberty, and the pursuit of organ sales', *Hastings Center Report*, 14 (1): 22–23.

Archard, D. (2002) 'Selling yourself: Titmuss's argument against a market in blood', *Journal of Ethics*, 6 (11): 87–103.

Arndt, E., Lefebvre, A., Travis, F. and Munro, I. (1986) 'Fact and fantasy: psychosocial consequences of facial surgery in 24 Down Syndrome children', *British Journal of Plastic Surgery*, 39 (4): 498–504.

Arrow, K. (1972) 'Gifts and exchanges', *Philosophy and Public Affairs*, 1 (4): 343–62.

Ashcroft, R. E., Campbell, A. V. and Jones, S. (2000) 'Solidarity, society and the welfare state in the United Kingdom', *Health Care Analysis*, 8 (4): 377–94.

Ashcroft, R. E., Dawson, A., Draper, H. and McMillan, J.R. (2007) *Principles of Health Care Ethics*, 2nd edn, Chichester, UK and Hoboken, NJ: John Wiley and Sons.

Awaya, T., Toledano, S. J., Siruno, L. H., Aguilar, F., Shimazono, Y. and de Castro, L. D. (forthcoming) Kidney transplantation in the Philippines: a survey of paid kidney donors'.

Barilan, Y. M. (2006) 'Body worlds and the ethics of using human remains: a preliminary discussion', *Bioethics*, 20 (5): 233–47.

Bartky, S. (1990) *Femininity and Domination: Studies in the Phenomenology of Oppression*, New York: Routledge.

Bataille, G. (1985) 'The language of flowers', *Visions of Excess: Selected Writings, 1927–1939*, trans. Allan Stoekl with Carl R. Lovitt and Donald M. Leslie, Jr., Minnesota: University of Minnesota Press.

Baudrillard, J. (1983) *Simulations*, New York: Semiotexte.

— (1993) *Symbolic Exchange and Death*, London: Sage Publications.

Baudrillard, J. and Witwer, J. (2000) *The Vital Illusion*, New York: Columbia University Press.

Bayh–Dole (1980) *35 U.S.C. §§200–211.*

Bayne, T. and Levy, L. (2005) 'Amputees by choice: body integrity identity disorder and the ethics of amputation', *Journal of Applied Philosophy*, 22 (1): 75–86.

Beauchamp, T. L. and Childress, J. F. (2009) *Principles of Biomedical Ethics*, 6th edn, New York: Oxford University Press.

Benatar, D. (2006) *Cutting to the Core: Exploring the Ethics of Contested Surgeries*, Lanham, MD: Rowman & Littlefield.

Benatar, S. (2004) 'Blinkered bioethics', *Journal of Medical Ethics*, 30 (3): 291–92.

Berlin, I. (1958) *Two Concepts of Liberty*, Oxford: Clarendon Press.

Berridge, V. (1997) 'AIDS and the gift relationship in the UK', in A. Oakley and J. Ashton (eds) *The Gift Relationship: From Human Blood to Social Policy*, original edition with new chapters, London: LSE Books.

Björkman, B. and Hansson, S. O. (2006) 'Bodily rights and property rights', *Journal of Medical Ethics*, 32: 209–14.

Bordo, S. (1993) *Unbearable Weight: Feminism, Western Culture, and the Body*, Berkeley, CA: University of California Press.

— (1997) 'Normalization and resistance in the era of the image', in S. Kemp and J. Squires (eds) *Feminisms*, New York: Oxford University Press.

— (1998) 'Reading the slender body', in D. Welton (ed.) *Body and Flesh: A Philosophical Reader*, Oxford: Blackwell.

Brazier, M. (2002) 'Retained organs: ethics and humanity', *Legal Studies*, 22 (4): 550–69.

— (2003) 'Organ retention and return: problems of consent', *Journal of Medical Ethics*, 29 (1): 30–33.

Brazier, M. and Cave, E. (2007) *Medicine, Patients and the Law*, 4th edn, London: Penguin Books.

Bristol Royal Infirmary Inquiry (2000) *Interim Report of the Bristol Royal Infirmary Inquiry*, London: Central Office of Information.

Brody, B. A. (2003) *Taking Issue: Pluralism and Casuistry in Bioethics*, Washington, DC: Georgetown University Press.

Broumand, B. (2005) 'Transplantation activities in Iran', *Experimental and Clinical Transplantation*, 3: 333–37.

Brown, D. E. (1991) *Human Universals*, New York: McGraw-Hill.

Brown, T. (2008) 'Strengthening blood systems in Africa: progress under PEPFAR and remaining challenges', *AABB News*. Available at http://www.aabb.org/Content/Programs_and_Services/Global_Initiatives/pepfarnews0408.htm (accessed 2 August 2008).

Burton, J. L. and Underwood, J. C. E. (2003) 'Necropsy practice after the "Organ Retention Scandal": requests, performance, and tissue retention', *Journal of Clinical Pathology*, 56 (7): 537–41.

Butler, J. (1990) *Gender Trouble*, New York and London: Routledge.

Campbell, A. V. (1986) *The Gospel of Anger*, London: SPCK.

— (2007) 'The ethical challenges of genetic databases: safeguarding altruism and trust', *King's Law Journal*, 18: 227–45.

Campbell, A. V., McLean, S. A., Gutridge, K. and Harper, H. (2008) 'Human tissue legislation: listening to the professionals', *Journal of Medical Ethics*, 34: 104–08.

Campbell, A. V. and Willis, M. (2005) 'They stole my baby's soul: narratives of embodiment and loss', *Medical Humanities*, 31 (2): 101–04.

Chief Medical Officer's Summit on Organ Retention (2001) *Evidence Documentation*, London: Department of Health.

Cohen, L. (1999) 'Where it hurts: Indian material for an ethics of organ transplantation', *Daedalus*, 128: 135–65.

Colorado State University Research Foundation (2006) 'What is Bayh–Dole and why is it important to technology transfer?' Available at http://www.csurf.org/enews/bayhdole_403.html (accessed 22 June 2008).

Cooper, M. H. and Culyer, A. J. (1973) 'The economics of giving and selling blood', in A. A. Alchian, W. R. Allen, G. Tullock, A. J. Culyer, T. R. Ireland, D. B. Johnson, M. H. Cooper, J. V. Koch, M. J. Ireland and A. J. Salisbury, *The Economics of Charity*, London: Institute of Economic Affairs.

Council of Europe (1999) *Organ Shortage: Current Status and Strategies for the Improvement of Organ Donation – A European Consensus Document*. Online. Available at http://www.edqm.eu/medias/fichiers/Organ_shortagecurrent_status_and_strategies_for_improvement_of_organ_donation_A_European_consensus_document.pdf (accessed 22 July 2008).

Council on Ethical and Judicial Affairs, American Medical Association (2002) 'Financial incentives for organ donation', in *Code of Medical Ethics: Current Opinions with Annotations*, Opinion 2.15, Chicago: American Medical Association.

Damasio, A. R. (1994) *Descartes' Error: Emotion, Reason, and the Human Brain*, New York: G. P. Putnam.

— (1999) *The Feeling of What Happens: Body and Emotion in the Making of Consciousness*, New York: Harcourt Brace.

Danto, A. (2002) 'The abuse of beauty', *Daedalus*, 131 (4): 35–56.

Dariotis, J., MacPherson, J. and Bianco, C. (2001) 'America's blood centers and the gift relationship', *Transfusion*, 41 (10): 1181–84.

Davis, K. (1995) *Reshaping the Female Body: The Dilemma of Cosmetic Surgery*, New York: Routledge.

— (1999) 'Cosmetic surgery in a different voice: the case of Madame Noël', *Women's Studies International Forum*, 22 (5): 473–88.

de Beauvoir, S. (1959) *A Very Easy Death*, New York: Pantheon Books.

de Castro, L. (2003) 'Commodification and exploitation: arguments in favour of compensated organ donation', *Journal of Medical Ethics*, 29: 142–46.

Devettere, R. J. (2000) *Practical Decision Making in Health Care Ethics: Cases and Concepts*, Washington, DC: Georgetown University Press.

Diamond v. Chakrabarty (1980) *447 U.S. 303*. US Supreme Court.

Dickenson, D. (2007) *Property in the Body: Feminist Perspectives*, Cambridge and New York: Cambridge University Press.

Draper, H. (2000) 'Anorexia nervosa and respecting a refusal of life-prolonging therapy: a limited justification,' *Bioethics*, 14 (2): 120–33.

— (2003) 'Anorexia nervosa and refusal of naso-gastric treatment: a reply to Simona Giordano', *Bioethics*, 17 (3): 279–89.

Draper, H. and Evans, N. (2006) 'Transsexualism and gender reassignment surgery', in D. Benatar (ed.) *Cutting to the Core: Exploring the Ethics of Contested Surgeries*, Lanham, MD: Rowman & Littlefield.

Duker, M. and Slade, R. (2002) *Anorexia Nervosa and Bulimia: How to Help*, London: Open University Press.

Dyer, C. (2000) 'Surgeon amputated healthy legs', *British Medical Journal*, 320 (7231): 332.

Eagleton, T. (1996) *The Illusions of Postmodernism*, Cambridge, MA: Blackwell Publishers.

Eco, U. (2007) *On Ugliness*, trans. Alastair McEwen, New York: Rizzoli International.

ECPAT (2005) *Combating Child Sex Tourism: Questions and Answers*. Available at http://www.ecpat.net/EI/PDF/CST/CST_FAQ_ENG.pdf (accessed 18 May 2008).

Elliott, C. (2003) *Better than Well: American Medicine Meets the American Dream*, New York and London: W. W. Norton and Company.

Emson, H. E. (2003) 'It is immoral to require consent for cadaver organ donation', *Journal of Medical Ethics*, 29: 125–27.

Erin, C. A. and Harris, J. (2003) 'An ethical market in human organs', *Journal of Medical Ethics*, 29: 137–38.

Faden, R. R. and Beauchamp, T. L. (1986) *A History and Theory of Informed Consent*, New York: Oxford University Press.

Farrell, A. M. (2006) 'Is the gift still good? Examining the politics and regulation of blood safety in the European Union', *Medical Law Review*, 14 (2): 155–79.

Fennell, S. and Jones, D. G. (1992) 'The bequest of human bodies for dissection: a case study in the Otago Medical School', *New Zealand Medical Journal*, 105: 472–74.

Finkelstein, P. and Mathers, L. (1990) 'Post traumatic stress among medical students in the anatomy dissection laboratory', *Clinical Autonomy*, 3: 219–26.

First, M. (2004) 'Desire for amputation of a limb: paraphilia, psychosis, or a new type of identity disorder', *Psychological Medicine*, 35: 919–28.

Foucault, M. (1975) *The Birth of the Clinic: An Archaeology of Medical Perception*, trans. A. M. Sheridan Smith, New York: Vintage Books.

Freud, S. (1961) *The Ego and the Id*, New York: Norton.

Friedman, A. L. (2006) 'Payment for living organ donation should be legalised', *British Medical Journal*, 333: 746–48.

Genelex Corporation (2008) *DNA Testing Experts for Paternity Testing, Ancestry & Pharmacogenetics*. Available at http://www.healthanddna.com/ (accessed 10 August 2008).

Ghods, A. J. and Savaj, S. (2006) 'Iranian model of paid and regulated living – unrelated kidney donation', *Clinical Journal of the American Society of Nephrology*, 1: 1136–45.

Ghods, A. J., Ossareh, S. and Khosravani, P. (2001) 'Comparison of some socio-economic characteristics of donors and recipients in a controlled living unrelated donor renal transplantation program', *Transplantation Proceedings*, 3: 2626–27.

Gill, M. B. and Sade, R. M. (2002) 'Paying for kidneys: the case against prohibition', *Kennedy Institute of Ethics Journal*, 12: 17–45.

Gimlin, D. (2002) 'Cosmetic surgery: paying for your beauty', in D. Gimlin (ed.) *Body Work: Beauty and Self-image in American Culture*, Berkeley, CA: University of California Press.

Giordano, S. (2003) 'Anorexia nervosa and refusal of naso-gastric treatment: a response to Heather Draper', *Bioethics*, 17 (3): 261–78.

—— (2005) *Understanding Eating Disorders: Conceptual and Ethical Issues in the Treatment of Anorexia and Bulimia Nervosa*, Oxford: Oxford University Press.

Glannon, W. (2008) 'Underestimating the risk in living kidney donation', *Journal of Medical Ethics*, 34: 127–28.

Glynn, S. A., Williams, A. E., Nass, C. C., Bethel, J., Kessler, D., Scott, E. P., Fridey, J., Kleinman, S. H. and Schreiber, G. B. (2003) 'Attitudes toward blood donation incentives in the United States: implications for donor recruitment', *Transfusion*, 43: 7–16.

Goeke, J., Kassow, D., May, D. and Kundert, D. (2003) 'Parental opinions about facial plastic surgery for individuals with Down syndrome', *Mental Retardation*, 41 (1): 29–34.

Gordon, R. (1990) *Anorexia and Bulimia: Anatomy of a Social Epidemic*, Cambridge, MA: Blackwell.

Goyal, M., Mehta, R. L., Schneiderman, L. J. and Sehgal, A. R. (2002) 'Economic and health consequences of selling a kidney in India', *Journal of the American Medical Association*, 288: 1589–93.

Greenberg v. Miami Children's Hospital Research Institute, Inc. (2003) 264 F. Supp. 2nd 1064 (S.D. Fla.).

Griffin, A. (2007) 'Kidneys on demand', *British Medical Journal*, 334: 502–05.

Hafferty, F. W. (1991) *Into the Valley: Death and the Socialization of Medical Students*, New Haven, CT: Yale University Press.

Haiken, E. (1997) *Venus Envy: A History of Cosmetic Surgery*, Baltimore, MD: Johns Hopkins University Press.

Haraway, D. (1997) 'A manifesto for cyborgs: science, technology, and socialist feminism in the 1980s', in D. T. Meyers (ed.) *Feminist Social Thought*, New York: Routledge.

Harding, S. (2006) *Science and Social Inequality: Feminist and Postcolonial Issues*, Urbana, IL and Chicago: University of Illinois Press.

Harris, J. (1985) *The Value of Life*, London and Boston, MA: Routledge and Kegan Paul.

— (1992) *Wonderwoman and Superman: The Ethics of Human Biotechnology*, Oxford and New York: Oxford University Press.

— (2002) 'Law and regulation of retained organs: the ethical issue', *Legal Studies*, 22: 527–49.

Hartsock, N. (1983) 'The feminist standpoint', in S. Harding and M. Hintikka (eds) *Discovering Reality*, London: D. Riedel Publishing Company.

Healy, K. (2000) 'Embedded altruism: blood collection regimes and the European Union's donor population', *American Journal of Sociology*, 105: 1633–57.

— (2006) 'Do presumed consent laws raise organ procurement rates?', *DePaul Law Review*, 55: 1017–43.

Herbert, F. (1968) *Dune*, London: New English Library.

Herring, J. and Chau, P. L. (2007) 'My body, your body, our bodies', *Medical Law Review*, 15: 34–61.

HM Inspector of Anatomy (2003) *Isaacs Report: The Investigation of Events that Followed the Death of Cyril Mark Isaacs*, London: Stationery Office.

hooks, b. (1982) 'Black women and feminism', in *Ain't I A Woman?*, London: Pluto Press.

Honoré, T. (1961) 'Ownership', in A. G. Guest (ed.) *Oxford Essays in Jurisprudence: A Collaborative Work*, London: Oxford University Press.

Horrobin, S. (2005) 'Review of stakes and kidneys: why markets in human body parts are morally imperative', *Rejuvenation Research*, 8: 258–63.

Human Fertilisation and Embryology Authority (HFEA) (2007) *Statement on Donating Eggs for Research*. Available at www.hfea.gov.uk (accessed 23 May 2008).

Human Genetics Commission (2002) *Inside Information: Balancing Interests in the Use of Personal Genetic Data*. Available at http://www.hgc.gov.uk/Client/document. asp?DocId = 131andCAtegoryId = 10 (accessed 13 May 2008).

Hume, D. (1911) *A Treatise of Human Nature*, London, New York: J. M. Dent and Sons.

Hunter, K. M. (1991) *Doctors' Stories: The Narrative Structure of Medical Knowledge*, Princeton, NJ: Princeton University Press.

Hwang, W. S., Ryu, Y. J., Park, J. H., Park, E. S., Lee, E. G., Koo, J. M., Jeon, H. Y., Lee, B. C., Kang, S. K., Kim, S. J., Ahn, C., Hwang, J. H., Park, K. Y., Cibelli, J. B. and Moon, S. Y. (2004) 'Evidence of a pluripotent human embryonic stem cell line derived from a cloned blastocyst', *Science Online*, 303: 1669–74.

Jakobsen, A. (1996) 'Living renal donors: the Norwegian experience', *Transplantation Proceedings*, 28: 3581.

Jakobsen, A., Holdaas, H. and Leivestad, T. (2003) 'Ethics and safety of living kidney donation', *Transplantation Proceedings*, 35 (3): 1177–78.

Jaye, C. (2004) 'Talking around embodiment: the views of GPs following participation in medical anthropology courses', *Medical Humanities*, 30: 41–48.

Johnston, J. and Elliott, C. (2002) 'Healthy limb amputation: ethical and legal aspects', *Clinical Medicine*, 2 (5): 431–35.

Jones, D. G. (2000) *Speaking for the Dead: Cadavers in Biology and Medicine*, Aldershot, Hants and Brookfield, VT: Ashgate.

— (2002) 'Reinventing anatomy: the impact of plastination on how we see the human body', *Clinical Anatomy*, 15: 436–40.

Jones, R. (2000) 'Parental consent to cosmetic facial surgery in Down's syndrome', *Journal of Medical Ethics*, 26: 101–2.

Joralemon, D. and Cox, P. (2003) 'Body values: the case against compensating for transplant organs', *Hastings Center Report*, 33 (1): 27–33.

Josefson, D. (2002) 'AMA considers whether to pay for donation of organs', *British Medical Journal*, 324 (7533): 1541.

Kant, I. (1965) *Critique of Pure Reason*, trans. Norman Kemp Smith, New York: St Martin's Press.

Karp, M. and Stoller, D. (1999) *The Bust Guide to the New Girl Order*, New York: Penguin Books.

Kass, L. (1985) *Toward a More Natural Science: Biology and Human Affairs*, New York: Free Press.

Kaye, J., Helgason, H. H., Nõmper, A., Sild, T. and Wendel, L. (2004) 'Population genetic databases: A comparative analysis of the law in Iceland, Sweden, Estonia and the UK', *Trames: Journal of the Humanities and Social Sciences*, 8: 15–33.

Kazantzakis, N. (1965) *Report to Greco*, New York: Simon and Schuster.

Kissell, J. L. (2000) 'The search for the meaning of the human body', in D. C. Thomasma and J. L. Kissell (eds) *The Health Care Professional as Friend and Healer: Building on the Work of Edmund D. Pellegrino*, Washington, DC: Georgetown University Press.

Klaiman, P. and Arndt, E. (1989) 'Facial reconstruction in Down syndrome: perceptions of the results by parents and normal adolescents', *Cleft Palate Journal*, 26 (3): 186–90.

Klinkum rechts der Isar Munich (2008) 'World's first transplant of both arms', *ScienceDaily*, 4 August. Available at http://www.sciencedaily.com/releases/2008/08/080801100431.htm (accessed 4 August 2008).

Kluge, E. H. (2000) 'Improving organ retrieval rates: various proposals and their ethical validity', *Health Care Analysis*, 8: 279–95.

Kramer, P. (2006) *The Blood of Government: Race, Empire, the United States, & the Philippines*, Chapel Hill: University of North Carolina Press.

Kravetz, S., Weller, A., Tennenbaum, R., Tzuriel, D. and Mintzker, Y. (1992) 'Plastic surgery on children with Down syndrome: parents' perceptions of physical, personal, and social functioning', *Research in Developmental Disabilities*, 13 (2): 145–56.

Kuczynski, A. (2006) *Beauty Junkie: Inside Our $15 Billion Obsession with Cosmetic Surgery*, New York: Doubleday.

Kuhse, H. and Singer, P. (1985) *Should the Baby Live? The Problem of Handicapped Infants*, Oxford: Oxford University Press.

Larkin, P. (1988) *Deceptions, Collected Poems*, London: The Marvell Press.

Leder, D. (1990) *The Absent Body*, Chicago: University of Chicago Press.

Levi-Strauss, C. (1968) *Structural Anthropology*, London: Allen Lane/The Penguin Press.

The Lives of Others (2006) motion picture, Lionsgate, UK.

Lloyd, G. (1986) *The Man of Reason: 'Male' and 'Female' in Western Philosophy*, London: Routledge.

Locke, J. (1986) *The Second Treatise on Civil Government* (first published in Two Treatises of Government [1690]), Buffalo, NY: Prometheus Books.

Longino, H. E. (1990) *Science as Social Knowledge: Values and Objectivity in Scientific Inquiry*, Princeton, NJ: Princeton University Press.

— (2002) *The Fate of Knowledge*, Princeton, NJ: Princeton University Press.

Lozanoff, S. (2002) 'Re-inventing anatomy: the impact of plastination on how we see the human body', *Clinical Anatomy*, 15 (6): 441–42.

Mack, E. (1989) 'Dominos and the fear of commodification', in J. W. Chapman and J. R. Pennock (eds) *Markets and Justice, Nomos XXXI*, New York: New York University Press.

Macklin, R. (2003) 'Dignity is a useless concept', *British Medical Journal*, 327: 1419–20.

— (2004) 'Reflections on the human dignity symposium: is dignity a useless concept?', *Journal of Palliative Care*, 20 (3): 212–16.

Mahoney, J. D. (2000) 'The market for human tissue', *Virginia Law Review*, 86 (2): 163–223.

Malinowski, B. (1922) *Argonauts of the Western Pacific: An Account of Native Enterprise and Adventure in the Archipelagoes of Melanesian New Guinea*, London and New York: G. Routledge and Sons/E. P. Dutton and Co.

— (1926) *Crime and Custom in Savage Society*, London: Routledge and Kegan Paul.

Matesanz, R. (2001) 'A decade of continuous improvement in cadaveric organ donation: the Spanish model', *Nefrologia*, 21 (Supp. 5): 59–67.

— (2003) 'Factors influencing the adaptation of the Spanish model of organ donation', *Transplant International*, 16: 736–41.

— (2004) 'Factors that influence the development of an organ donation program', *Transplantation Proceedings*, 36: 739–41.

Mauss, M. (1954) *The Gift: Forms and Functions of Exchange in Archaic Societies*, Glencoe, IL: Free Press.

Mayrhofer-Reinhartshuber, D., Fitzgerald, A., Benetka, G. and Fitzgerald, R. (2006) 'Effects of financial incentives on the intention to consent to organ donation: a questionnaire survey', *Transplantation Proceedings*, 38: 2756–60.

McLachlan, J. C., Bligh, J., Bradley, P. and Searle, J. (2004) 'Teaching anatomy without cadavers', *Medical Education*, 38: 418–24.

Merleau-Ponty, M. (1962) *Phenomenology of Perception*, trans. Colin Smith, rev. edn (2002) London: Routledge.

Meyer, M. L. (2005) *Thicker than Water: The Origins of Blood as Symbol and Ritual*, New York: Routledge.

Miah, A. and Rich, E. (2008) *The Medicalization of Cyberspace*, London and New York: Routledge.

Michel, A., Mormont, C. and Legros, J. (2001) 'A psycho-endocrinological overview of transsexualism', *European Journal of Endocrinology*, 145: 365–76.

Mill, J. S. (1989) '*On Liberty, with The Subjection of Women, and Chapters on Socialism*', S. Collini (ed.), Cambridge and New York: Cambridge University Press.

Miller, P. (ed.) (2006), *Better Humans? The Politics of Human Enhancement and Life Extension*, London: Demos.

Money, J., Jobaris, R. and Furth, G. (1977) 'Apotemnophilia: two cases of self-demand amputation as a paraphilia', *Journal of Sex Research*, 13 (2): 115–25.

Moore v. Regents of the University of California (1990) *51 Cal. 3d 120, 793 P.2d 479, 271 Cal. Rptr. 146*.

Morris, J. (2002) *Conundrum*, New York: New York Review of Books.

Morriss-Kay, G. (2002) 'Review of body worlds', *Journal of Anatomy*, 200 (5): 535–36.

Mueller, L. (2007) 'Illogical desires that can't be ignored', *Toronto Star*, 4 October.

Mueller, S. (2007) 'Amputee envy', *Scientific American* (December 2007/January 2008): 60–65.

Murray, T. H. (1987) 'Gifts of the body and the needs of strangers', *Hastings Center Report*, 17: 30–38.

— (1992) 'The moral repugnance of rewarded gifting', *Transplantation and Immunology Letter*, 8 (1): 5–7.

National Commission for the Protection of Human Subjects of Biomedical and Behavioral Research (1979) *The Belmont Report: Ethical Principles and Guidelines for the Protection of Human Subjects of Research*, Washington, DC: US Government Printing Office.

National Health Service (2007) *UK Transplant Activity Report 2006–2007*. Available at http://www.uktransplant.org.uk/ukt/statistics/transplant_activity_report/current_activity_reports/ukt/transplant_activity_uk_2006–2007.pdf (accessed 4 July 2008).

Nuffield Council on Bioethics (2007) *The Forensic Use of Bioinformation: Ethical Issues*. Available at http://www.nuffieldbioethics.org/go/ourwork/bioinformationuse/publication_441.html (accessed 11 August 2008).

O'Neill, K. (2003) 'A vital fluid: risk, controversy and the politics of blood donation in the era of "Mad Cow Disease"', *Public Understanding of Science*, 12: 359–80.

O'Neill, O. (2002) *Autonomy and Trust in Bioethics*, Cambridge and New York: Cambridge University Press.

Pellegrino, E. D. and Thomasma, D. C. (1993) *The Virtues in Medical Practice*, New York: Oxford University Press.

Post, S. G. and Binstock, R. H. (2004) *The Fountain of Youth: Cultural, Scientific, and Ethical Perspectives on a Biomedical Goal*, New York: Oxford University Press.

President's Council on Bioethics (2008) *Human Dignity and Bioethics*, Washington, DC. Available at http://www.bioethics.gov/reports/human_dignity/index.html (accessed 2 August 2008).

Qiu, R. (2004) *Bioethics – Asian Perspectives: A Quest for Moral Diversity*, Dordrecht and Boston, MA: Kluwer Academic Publishers.

Radcliffe-Richards, J., Daar, A. S., Guttmann, R. D., Hoffenberg, R., Kennedy, I., Lock, M., Sells, R. A. and Tilney, N. (1998) 'The case for allowing kidney sales. International forum for transplant ethics', *Lancet*, 351: 1950–52.

Radin, M. J. (1996) *Contested Commodities*, Cambridge, MA: Harvard University Press.

Ramachandran, V. and McGeoch, P. (2007) 'Can vestibular caloric stimulation be used to treat apotemnophilia?', *Medical Hypotheses*, 69 (2): 250–52.

Raymond, J. (1979) *The Transsexual Empire*, London: Women's Press.

Rees, M. (1999) *Just Six Numbers: The Deep Forces that Shape the Universe*, New York: Basic Books.

Retained Organs Commission (2002) *Proposals for Identifying and Meeting Families' Support Needs*, Annex 1, Outline tender specification document: Identifying and meeting the support needs of families affected by organ retention, ninth meeting, 30 May.

Richardson, R. (1987) *Death, Dissection, and the Destitute*, London and New York: Routledge and Kegan Paul.

Riley, D. (1988) *Am I that Name? Feminism and the Category of 'Women' in History*, New York: Macmillan.

Robinson, D. and Medlock, N. (2005) 'Diamond v. Chakrabarty: a retrospective on 25 years of biotech patents', *Intellectual Property and Technology Law Journal*, 17: 12–15.

Rothman, D. J. (2002) 'Ethical and social consequences of selling a kidney', *Journal of American Medical Association*, 288: 1640–41.

Royal Liverpool Children's Inquiry (2001) *Report of the Royal Liverpool Children's Inquiry*, London: Stationery Office.

Rudge, C. (2003) 'Transplantation of organs natural limitations, possible solutions – a UK perspective', *Transplantation Proceedings*, 35 (3): 1149–50.

Ryle, G. (1949) *The Concept of Mind*, London: Hutchinson.

Sacks, O. (1985) *The Man Who Mistook His Wife for a Hat*, London: Duckworth.

Sanz, A., Boni, R. C., Ghirardini, A., Costa, A. N. and Manyalich, M. (2007) 'IRODaT 2006. International donation and transplantation activity', *Organs and Tissues and Cells*, 2: 77–80.

Sauer, M. V. (2001) 'Defining the incidence of serious complications experienced by oocyte donors: a review of 1000 cases', *American Journal of Obstetrics and Gynecology*, 184: 277–78.

Savulescu, J. (2003) 'Is the sale of body parts wrong?', *Journal of Medical Ethics*, 29: 138–39.

Sawday, J. (1995) *The Body Emblazoned: Dissection and the Human Body in Renaissance Culture*, London and New York: Routledge.

Scarry, E. (1987) *The Body in Pain: the Making and Unmaking of the World*, Oxford: Oxford University Press.

Scheper-Hughes, N. (2003) 'Rotten trade: millennial capitalism, human values and global justice in organs trafficking', *Journal of Human Rights*, 2: 197–226.

— (2006) 'Alistair Cooke's bones: a morality tale', *Anthropology Today*, 22: 3–8.

Scheper-Hughes, N. and Lock, M. (1987) 'The mindful body: a prolegomenon to future work in medical anthropology', *Medical Anthropology Quarterly*, 1 (1): 6–41.

Schuind, F., Abramowicz, D. and Schneeberger, S. (2007) 'Hand transplantation: the state-of-the-art', *Journal of Hand Surgery* (European volume), 32: 2–17.

Schwartz, J. (1999) 'Blood and altruism – Richard Titmuss' criticism on the commercialization of blood', *Public Interest*, 68 (1): 35–51.

Seale, C., Kirk, D., Tobin, M., Burton, P., Grundy, R., Pritchard-Jones, K. and Dixon-Woods, M. (2005) 'Effect of media portrayals of removal of children's tissue on UK tumour bank', *British Medical Journal*, 331: 401–03.

Shannon, R. (1975) *The Peacock and the Phoenix*, Millbrae, CA: Celestial Arts.

Shearmur, J. (2001) 'Trust, Titmuss and blood', *Institute of Economic Affairs*, 21 (1): 29–33.

Shildrick, M. (1997) *Leaky Bodies and Boundaries: Feminism, Postmodernism and (Bio)ethics*, London and New York: Routledge.

Shildrick, M. and Mykitiuk, R. (2005) *Ethics of the Body: Postconventional Challenges*, Cambridge, MA: MIT Press.

Shimazono, Y. (2007) 'The state of the international organ trade: a provisional picture based on integration of available information', *Bulletin of the World Health Organization*, 85: 955–62.

Sidgwick, H. (1891) *The Elements of Politics*, London: Macmillan.

Simpson, B. (2004) 'Impossible gifts: bodies, Buddhism and bioethics in contemporary Sri Lanka', *Journal of the Royal Anthropological Institute*, 10: 839–59.

Singer, P. (1993) *Practical Ethics*, Cambridge and New York: Cambridge University Press.

— (1995) *Rethinking Life and Death: The Collapse of our Traditional Ethics*, New York: Oxford University Press.

Singh, D. (2003) 'Scientist or Showman?', *British Medical Journal*, 326: 468.

Skegg, P. D. (1974) 'Liability for the unauthorized removal of cadaveric transplant material', *Medicine, Science and the Law*, 14 (1): 53–57.

— (1988) *Law, Ethics and Medicine*, rev. edn, Oxford: Clarendon Press/Oxford University Press.

— (1991) 'The use of corpses for medical education and research: the legal requirements', *Medicine, Science and the Law*, 31: 345–54.

— (1992) 'Criminal liability for the unauthorized use of corpses for medical education and research', *Medicine, Science and the Law*, 32: 51–54.

Skjøld, R. (2004) 'Xenotransplantation – view of the transplanted patient', *Acta Veterinaria Scandinavica*, 45 (Supp. 1): S59–S63.

Slynkova, K., Mannino, D. M., Martin, G. S., Morehead, R. S. and Doherty, D. E. (2006) 'The role of body mass index and diabetes in the development of acute organ failure and subsequent mortality in an observational cohort', *Critical Care*, 10: R137. Available at http://ccforum.com/content/10/5/R137 (accessed 5 August 2008).

Snowdon, C., Elbourne, D. R. and Garcia, J. (2004) 'Perinatal pathology in the context of a clinical trial: attitudes of neonatologists and pathologists', *Archives of Disease in Childhood Fetal and Neonatal Editio*, 89 (3): F204–F207.

Steering Committee of the Istanbul Summit (2008a) 'Organ trafficking and transplant tourism and commercialism: the Declaration of Istanbul', *Lancet*, 372: 5–6.

— (2008b) *The Declaration of Istanbul on Organ Trafficking and Transplant Tourism*. Available at http://www.prnewswire.com/mnr/transplantationsociety/33914/docs/33914-Declaration_of_Istanbul-Lancet.pdf (accessed 7 July 2008).

Steinbrook, R. (2006) 'Egg donation and human embryonic stem-cell research', *New England Journal of Medicine*, 354: 324–26.

Steiner, P. (2003/5) 'Gifts of blood and organs: the market and "fictitious commodities"', *Revue française de sociologie*, 44: 147–62.

Stolnitz, J. (1961) 'Beauty: some stages in the history of an idea', *Journal of the History of Ideas*, 22 (2): 185–204.

Swain, M. S. and Marusyk, R. W. (1990) 'An alternative to property rights in human tissue', *Hastings Center Report*, 20 (5): 12–15.

Sykora, P. (forthcoming) 'Altruism in medical donations reconsidered: the reciprocity approach', in M. Steinmann, P. Sykora and U. Wiesing (eds) *Altruism Reconsidered: Exploring New Approaches to Property in Human Tissue*, Aldershot: Ashgate Publishing Limited.

Shakespeare, W. (2006) *The Complete Plays and Sonnets of William Shakespeare (38 Volume Library) By William Shakespeare*, S. Orgel and A. R. Braunmiller (eds), London: Penguin.

Tagore, R. (1914) *Gitanjali (Song Offerings). A Collection of Prose Translations Made by the Author from the Original Bengali*, New York: Macmillan.

Taub, S., Maixner, A. H., Morin, K. and Sade, R. M. (2003) 'Cadaveric organ donation: encouraging the study of motivation', *Transplantation*, 76: 748–51.

Thomas, D. (1971) *The Poems*, London: Dent.

Tillich, P. (1963) *The Eternal Now*, New York: Scribner.

Titmuss, R. M. (1970) *The Gift Relationship: From Human Blood to Social Policy*, London: George Allen and Unwin.

Tong, R. (1997) *Feminist Approaches to Bioethics: Theoretical Reflections and Practical Applications*, Boulder, CO: Westview Press.

Tong, R. and Lindemann, H. (2006) 'Beauty under the knife: a feminist appraisal of cosmetic surgery', in D. Benatar, *Cutting to the Core: Exploring the Ethics of Contested Surgeries*, Lanham, MD: Rowman & Littlefield.

UK Biobank (2007) *Biobank: Improving the Health of Future Generations*. Available at http://www.ukbiobank.ac.uk/ (accessed 23 July 2008).

UN (1948) *Universal Declaration of Human Rights*, G.A. res. 217A (III), U.N. Doc A/810 at 71.

—— (1983) *Decade of Disabled Persons 1983–1992, World Programme of Action Concerning Disabled Persons*, New York: United Nations.

UNICEF (2005) *Trafficking for Sexual Exploitation and other Exploitative Purposes*. Innocenti Publications. Available at http://www.unicef-irc.org/cgi-bin/unicef/Lunga. sql?ProductID = 386 (accessed 1 July 2008).

United Network for Organ Sharing (2008) *U.S. Transplantation Data*. Online. Available at http://www.unos.org (accessed 22 July 2008).

U.S. Department of Health and Human Services, Health Resources and Services Administration, Office of Special Programs, Division of Transplantation (2003) *The Organ Donation Breakthrough Collaborative: Best Practices Final Report*. Available at http://www.njha.com/onit/pdf/930200530512PM71.pdf (accessed 9 August 2008).

U.S. Organ Procurement and Transplantation Network and the Scientific Registry of Transplant Recipients (2007) *Report on Transplant Data 1997–2006*. Available at http://www.optn.org/AR2007/default.htm (accessed 7 August 2008).

Veatch, R. M. (2003) 'Why liberals should accept financial incentives for organ procurement', *Kennedy Institute of Ethics Journal*, 13: 19–36.

von Hagens, G. (2006/07) *Body Worlds – The Original Exhibition of Real Human Bodies*, Institute for Plastination, Heidelberg, Germany. Available at www.bodyworlds. com (accessed 9 August 2008).

Waldby, C. (2008) 'Oocyte markets: women's reproductive work in embryonic stem cell research', *New Genetics and Society*, 27: 19–31.

Waldby, C. and Mitchell, R. (2006) *Tissue Economies: Blood, Organs, and Cell Lines in Late Capitalism*, Durham, NC: Duke University Press.

Waldron, J. (1987) *"Nonsense upon stilts": Bentham, Burke, and Marx on the Rights of Man*, London and New York: Methuen.

Waliur, R. (2008) 'Dhaka woman offers eye for sale', *BBC News*, 20 April 2005. Available at http://news.bbc.co.uk/2/hi/south_asia/4466883.stm (accessed 4 August 2008).

Waltz, E. (2006) 'The body snatchers', *Nature Medicine*, 12: 487–88.

Weiglein, A. H. (2002) 'Letter to the editor: preservation and plastination', *Clinical Anatomy*, 15: 445.

Weinberg, P. D., Hounshell, J., Sherman, L. A., Godwin, J., Ali, S., Tomori, C. and Bennett, C. L. (2002) 'Legal, financial, and public health consequences of HIV contamination of blood and blood products in the 1980s and 1990s', *Annals of Internal Medicine*, 136: 312–19.

Weir, R. F. and Olick, R. S. (2004) *The Stored Tissue Issue: Biomedical Research, Ethics, and Law in the Era of Genomic Medicine*, New York: Oxford University Press.

Weiss, G. (1999) *Body Images: Embodiment as Intercorporeality*, New York and London: Routledge.

Wendell, S. (1996) *The Rejected Body: Feminist Philosophical Reflections on Disability*, New York: Routledge.

Wilkinson, S. (2000) 'Commodification arguments for the legal prohibition of organ sale', *Health Care Analysis*, 8: 189–201.

—— (2003) *Bodies for Sale: Ethics and Exploitation in the Human Body Trade*, London and New York: Routledge.

Winickoff, D. E. (2007) 'Partnership in U.K. biobank: a third way for genomic property?', *Journal of Law, Medicine and Ethics*, 35: 440–56.

Wittig, M. (1992 [1981]) 'One is not born a woman', in *The Straight Mind*, Hemel Hempstead: Harvester Wheatsheaf.

Wolf, N. (1991) *The Beauty Myth: How Images of Beauty Are Used Against Women*, New York: William Morrow.

World Health Organization (WHO) (2003) *Malaria and HIV/AIDS Interactions and Implications*. Available at http://www.who.int/malaria/malaria_HIV/malaria_hiv_fly er.pdf (accessed 1 July 2008).

—— (2007) *International Statistical Classification of Diseases and Related Health Problems 10th Revision*, Geneva. Available at http://www.who.int/classifications/ apps/icd/icd10online/ (accessed 11 August 2008).

—— (2008a) *Blood Safety and Donation*. Available at http://www.who.int/mediacentre /factsheets/fs279/en/index.html (accessed 1 July 2008).

—— (2008b) *Guiding Principles on Human Cell, Tissue and Organ Transplantation*. Available at http://www.who.int/transplantation/TxGP08-en.pdf (accessed 8 July 2008).

Yu, W. (2008) 'The management for blood safety in China', *ISBT Science Series*, 3: 68–70.

Zhang, L., Li, Y., Zhou, J., Miao, X., Wang, G., Li, D., Nielson, K., Long, Y. and Li, J. (2007) 'Knowledge and willingness toward living organ donation: a survey of three universities in Changsha, Hunan Province, China', *Transplantation Proceedings*, 39: 1303–9.

Zimrin, A. B. and Hess, J. R. (2007) 'Blood donors and the challenges in supplying blood products and factor concentrates', *Surgery*, 142: 15–19.

Index

accountability and openness 70–71
adverse selection problem 29
advertising 85, 88, 92
aesthetic surgery *see* cosmetic surgery/ medicine
Africa 36, 84
agape 22
ageing and death 93, 125
AIDS/HIV 29–30, 31, 36, 56
alienability: commodities 16–17; parts of body 13, 14, 15–16, 17–19, 46
altruism: autopsies 100–101; biobanks 66–71; donation of body for dissection 108; embedded 33; gift relationship 19–20; giving to unnamed strangers 20–21, 32–33; nature of 22–23; paid organ donation as threat to 43–46; purity of gift relationship 21–22; value(s) of the body and its parts 23–26
American Medical Association 53
amputation 76–77
anatomical dissection 3, 107–8; coronial autopsies 100, 110; public autopsies 103, 106; retained organs controversy 1–2, 96–103, 112; training of medical students 108–10
Anderson, E. 24–25
Andrews, L.B. 11, 15, 55, 56
Annas, G.J. 41
anorexia 79–80, 92
Antigone 113
Archard, D. 20, 21
Arndt, E. 82
Arrow, K. 32
Ashcroft, R.E. 3, 21
Asia 52
Asia-Pacific region 31

Australia 37, 116
Austria 43, 114
autonomy 42, 79
autopsies: coronial 100, 110; public 103, 106; retained organs controversy 1–2, 96–103, 112
Awaya, T. 27, 40, 42, 43

Bangladesh 31
Barilan, Y.M. 104–5, 106–7
Bartky, S. 86–87
Bataille, G. 129
Baudrillard, J. 88, 90–91, 93, 95
Bayh–Dole Act 1980 57, 58
Bayne, T. 76
Beauchamp, T.L. 3
beauty, fragility of 89–91
Benatar, S. 42
Bentham, J. 12, 103
Berlin, I. 17
Bible 115
BIID (body image disorder identity) 75–77
bio-piracy 56
biobanks 60, 66–67; independent oversight 69–70; openness and accountability 70–71; participation and partnership 67–69
biotechnology industry 61, 64–66; *see also* patents; tissue, human
Björkman, B. 12
blood: efficiency and effectiveness 28–29; embedded altruism 33; fractionization 60; in-principle argument 32; payment for 19–21, 28–33; quality control 29; safety 29–31; symbolic meaning and role of 28

body image disorder identity (BIID) 75–77
Body Worlds (*Körperwelten*) 103–7
Bolivia 37
Bordo, S. 85–86, 87, 87–88
brain dead 111–12
Brazier, M. 56, 100, 102–3, 113
Brazil 37
Brody, B.A. 3
Broumand, B. 50
Brown, D.E. 113
Brown, T. 31
bulimia 79–80
Burton, J.L. 110

Campbell, A.V. 67, 97, 99, 101
Canada 37, 116
Cartesian dualism 2, 4
cell lines *see* tissue, human
Chakrabarty case 57–58
charitable donor 22
charities, percentage of profits to 63, 73
Cher 88, 89
China 31, 35, 65, 84
clinical medicine, emergence of 3
coercion 42–43
Cohen, L. 42
commensurability 16–17, 46
commodification debate 16–19, 46–47
consent 72; living organ donors 41–43; oocytes for research 65; patients and sample body tissue 59–60; plastic surgery on children 83; presumed/opt out 113, 114; removal of organs after brain death 112–14; UK Biobank 60, 67
consequentialism 3–4
Cooke, Alistair 11
Cooper, M.H. 32
corneal transplants 47, 111
cosmetic surgery/medicine: aesthetic surgery 129; appearance and reality 87–89; body as 'ultimate fashion accessory' 83–84; Down syndrome children 82–83; empowerment 87; fragility of beauty 89–91; power of the image 85–86; subjugation 86–87
Crete 65
cyborgs 92

Damasio, A.R. 4–6
Danto, A. 89–90

Dariotis, J. 28
databases: biobanks 66–71; forensic DNA 70–71
Davis, K. 87
de Beauvoir, Simone 124
de Castro, L. 43–44
dead body 95–96; anatomical dissection 3, 99–101, 103, 106, 107–10; brain dead 111–12; consent to removal of organs 112–14; display of 103–7; funeral home viewing 93; gifts of memory 115–18; next of kin 13, 48, 52, 96–103, 112, 113, 114; retained organs controversy 1–2, 96–103, 112; transplantable organs from 13, 34, 47, 111–14
deaf community 81
Descartes, R. 2, 3
Devettere, R.J. 3
diabetes 36
Diamond v *Chakrabarty* 57–58
Dickenson, D. 62, 64, 65–66, 68, 72, 73
dignity, concept of 26
disabled people 81–83
disappearing body 7–9
discomfort of embodiment 75; alien body 75–77; conclusion 92–93; cosmetic surgery/medicine 83–91, 129; disability 81–83; eating disorders 79–80, 92; transsexualism 77–78
dissection, anatomical 3, 107–8; coronial autopsies 100, 110; public autopsies 103, 106; retained organs controversy 1–2, 96–103, 112; training of medical students 108–10
DNA databases, forensic 70–71
Down syndrome children 82–83
Draper, H. 77, 78, 79
dualism, Cartesian 2, 4
Duker, M. 80
Dune 112
Dyer, C. 76
dys-appearing body 7, 8–9, 75, 80

Eagleton, T. 122, 124
eating disorders 79–80
Economist 49, 51
eggs for research, human *see* oocytes for research
Elliott, C. 91, 121
embodied self 4–9, 18, 25, 93; property rights 15

emotion 5–6, 119
Emson, H.E. 112, 115
environment, dependency on 14–15,
    124–25
Erin, C.A. 16, 35, 36, 38, 44, 45
Europe: blood donations/market 29, 33
European Union: waiting lists for
    organs 35

Faden, R.R. 42
Farrell, A.M. 29–30
fashion 121–22; cosmetic surgery *see*
    cosmetic surgery/medicine
feminism 4, 6–7, 86–87, 92
Fennell, S. 109
Finkelstein, P. 109
First, M. 75, 76
forensic DNA databases 70–71
former Soviet bloc countries 65
Foucault, M. 3, 6
France 92; blood 30; kidney donations 51
freak shows 81, 105
free market *see* market economy
freedom 17, 42; conformity as 84
Freud, S. 125
Friedman, A.L. 39–40
fungibility 16–17, 46

gametes, market in 64
gender reassignment 77–78
Genesis 3:19 115
Ghods, A.J. 49, 50
gift relationship 19–20; biobanks 66–71;
    embedded altruism 33; giving to
    unnamed strangers 20–21, 32–33;
    nature of altruism 22–23; paid organ
    donation as threat to altruism 43–46;
    purity of 21–22; value(s) of the body
    and its parts 23–26
Gill, M.B. 47
Gimlin, D. 87
Giordano, S. 79–80
Glannon, W. 40
globalization 61, 64–66
Glynn, S.A. 31
Goeke, J. 82, 83
Gordon, R. 80
Goyal, M. 40
Griffin, A. 43, 49, 50, 51

Hafferty, F.W. 109
Haiken, E. 87

hand, replacement of severed 47
handicap, impairment and disability 81
Haraway, D. 92
Harris, J. 2, 3, 95, 96, 102, 112–13
Healy, K. 33, 52–53, 114
heart transplants 47
Herbert, Frank 112
Herring, J. 14
HIV/AIDS 29–30, 31, 36, 56
Honoré, T. 12–13, 14, 62
Horrobin, S. 41
human eggs for research *see* oocytes for
    research
'human non-subject research' (HNR)
    71–72
Hume, D. 3, 5
Hunter, K, M. 97
Hwang Woo Suk 63, 65

impairment, disability and handicap 81
in vitro fertilization 64
independent oversight 69–70
India 37, 40, 65
indigenous peoples 116–18
informational interconnectivity 61–63
insurance: organ donation 48–49
intellectual property *see* patents
Internet 37
Iran: legitimized market in organs 43,
    49–51
Israel 37
Istanbul Declaration 48, 49
Italy 92

Jakobsen, A. 52
Japan 37, 65
Jaye, C. 100
Johnston, J. 76
Jones, D.G. 102, 103, 104, 105, 107,
    108, 109, 110, 111–12, 116–17
Jones, R. 82
Joralemon, D. 41
Josefson, D. 53

Kant, I. 3, 9, 17, 18
Karp, M. 87
Kass, L. 57–58
Kaye, J. 68
Kazantzakis, N. 115
kidney donation, live 37–38; body
    commodification 16–19, 46–47;
    conclusion 53; consent 41–43;

contested solutions 48–49;
exploitation 38–40; harm and benefit
40–41; legitimized market: Iran
49–51; non-market solutions 51–53;
threat to altruism 43–46
kidney failure 34, 35
Kissell, J.L. 71–72
Klaiman, P. 83
Kluge, E.H. 27, 43
Korea 65
Kravetz, S. 83
Kuczynski, A. 84, 85

'leakiness' of bodies 6, 14, 123
Leder, D. 4, 7–8, 9, 75, 80
Lenin 103
Leonardo da Vinci 107
Levi-Strauss, C. 21
libertarianism 4
Lives of Others, The 122–23
Locke, J. 3, 12
Lozanoff, S. 105

Mack, E. 21
Macklin, R. 26
McLachlan, J.C. 109
Madonna 88
Mahoney, J.D. 16
malaria 36
Malinowski, B. 21
Maori 84, 116–17
market economy 16–19, 24, 27–28, 47;
blood, payment for 19–21, 28–33;
organs from living donors:
legitimized market in Iran 49–51
Mastromarino, Michael 56
Matesanz, R. 51–52
Matrix, The 88
Mauss, M. 21
Mayrhofer-Reinhartshuber, D. 43
medicine, emergence of clinical 3
Merleau-Ponty, M. 4, 6
Meyer, M.L. 28
Miah, A. 103, 106
Michel, A. 78
Mill, J.S. 4
Miller, P. 83
Money, J. 76
Moore v *The Regents of the University
of California* 16, 57, 58–60, 72
Morris, J. 77, 78
Morriss-Kay, G. 103, 104

Mueller, L. 77
Mueller, S. 76
Murray, T.H. 32, 45

Natural History Museum in London 116
natural rights approach to property 12
natural world 124–25
negative freedom 17
New Zealand Maori 84, 116–17
Noël, S. 87
Norway 52

Oman 37
O'Neill, K. 30
O'Neill, O. 42
oocytes for research 63; association
with reproduction 64, 65; global
trading 64–66; property rights 65–66;
quantity of 63–64; risks 64
openness and accountability 70–71
organ trade debate 34; body
commodification 16–19, 46–47;
conclusion 53; consent 41–43;
contested solutions 48–49;
exploitation 38–40; harm and benefit
40–41; hypocrisy 44, 45; legitimized
market: Iran 49–51; non-market
solutions 51–53; organ 'crisis' 34–35;
organ trafficking 37–38; scarcity
scepticism 35–37; threat to altruism
43–46; World Health Organization
48–49
organs, human: commodities 16–19,
46–47; dead body *see* dead body;
hospital as fiduciary 15; retained
organs controversy 1–2, 96–103, 112
otherness 81–82
oversight, independent 69–70

Pacific Island warriors 84
Padaung people 84
Pakistan 37
partnerships 67–69, 73
patents: Bayh–Dole Act 1980 57, 58;
Diamond v *Chakrabarty* 57–58;
Moore case 16, 57, 58–60, 72; UK
Stem Cell Bank 73
paternalism 39, 41, 43, 79
Pellegrino, E.D. 3
pharmacogenetics 66
phenomenology 6–7
Philippines 40, 44

plastination: *Body Worlds*
  (*Körperwelten*) 103–7
police DNA databases 70–71
post mortem examination 110; coroner
  100, 110; public 103, 106; retained
  organs controversy 1–2; 96–103, 112
Post, S.G. 95
pregnancy 14, 64
principlism 3
property, intellectual *see* patents
property paradigm 12; bundle of rights
  and obligations 12–14; distinction
  between whole and parts 15–16;
  human tissue 15–16, 56–60, 61,
  62–63; limitations of 14–15, 72;
  natural rights approach 12; oocytes
  for research 65–66; social
  constructivist approach 12

Qiu, R. 3

Radcliffe-Richards, J. 36, 38, 40
Radin, M.J. 16, 17–19, 24–25, 47
Ramachandran, V. 76
Raymond, J. 77
reciprocity 22–23
Red Crescent 31
Red Cross 31, 33
respect, concept of 26, 73, 123
Richardson, R. 3, 11, 103, 107, 108
risks: kidney donation 40, 41
Robinson, D. 61
Rothman, D.J. 42
Rudge, C. 52
Ryle, Gilbert 2

Sacks, Oliver 75–76
Sanz, A. 51
Saudi Arabia 37
Sauer, M.V. 64
Savulescu, J. 39
Sawday, J. 107–8
Scheper-Hughes, N. 4, 11, 27, 36, 46, 47
Schuind, F. 47
Schwartz, J. 29
science fiction 92
Seale, C. 97
Shakespeare, W. 93
Shannon, Robert 89
Shearmur, J. 29, 32
Shildrick, M. 6, 7, 14
Shimazono, Y. 37

Sidgwick, H. 13
Singapore 34
Singer, P. 3, 4
Singh, D. 105
Skegg, P.D. 56, 100
Skjøld, R. 52
slavery 17
Slynkova, K. 36
Snowdon, C. 110
social conformity 84, 87
social constructivist approach to
  property 12
South Africa 116
Southeast Asia 47
Spain 65; organ donation 51–52
Steinbrook, R. 63, 64
Steiner, P. 16
stem cells *see* tissue, human
Stolnitz, J. 89
Swain, M.S. 15–16
Sykora, P. 21–23, 24, 28–29

Tagore, Rabinranath 115
Tanzania 31
tattooing 84
Taub, S. 53
Thomas, Dylan 115
Tillich, P. 119
Times, The 97
tissue, human 55–56; accountability
  70–71; Bayh–Dole Act 1980 57, 58;
  biobanks 60, 66–71; *Chakrabarty*
  case 57–58; circulating value 61;
  common humanity 71–73;
  fractionalization and fragmentation
  60; globalization 61, 64–66;
  independent oversight 69–70;
  informational interconnectivity
  61–63; *Moore* case 16, 57, 58–60, 72;
  oocytes for research 63–66; openness
  70–71; partnerships 67–69, 73;
  percentage of profits to charities 63,
  73; property rights 15–16, 56–60, 61,
  62–63; World Health Organization
  48; *see also* blood; organs, human;
  trafficking in organs
Titmuss, R.M. 19–21, 22, 24, 28–29,
  32–33, 53, 61
Tong, R. 3, 85, 86, 87
trafficking in organs 37–38; body
  commodification 16–19, 46–47;
  consent 41–43; contested solutions

48–49; exploitation 38–40; harm and benefit 40–41; legitimized market: Iran 49–51; non-market solutions 51–53; organ 'crisis' 34–35; scarcity scepticism 35–37; threat to altruism 43–46; World Health Organization 48–49
transsexualism 77–78
Truman Show, The 88

United Kingdom: Biobank project 60, 67, 68–69; blood 29, 30, 61; kidney donations 51; Natural History Museum 116; police National DNA Database 70; public autopsy 103, 106; Stem Cell Bank 73; in vitro fertilization 64
United Nations 81
United States 116; American Medical Association 53; Bayh–Dole Act 1980 57, 58; bio-piracy 56; biotechnology industry 61, 65; cosmetic procedures 85; *Diamond* v *Chakrabarty* 57–58; elective post mortems 110; financial incentives 43; gametes, market in 64; kidney donations 49, 51; *Moore* case 16, 57, 58–60, 72; oocytes, market in research 64–65; organ donation rates 35; payment for blood 19–20, 28–29, 31, 61; waiting lists for organs 34–35

values: monistic view of 23, 24; plurality of 23–26
variant Creutzfeldt–Jakob disease (vCJD) 30
Veatch, R.M. 39, 40, 45
voluntariness 42–43
von Donnersmarck, Florian Henckel 122
von Hagens, Gunther 103–7

Waldby, C. 16, 26, 28, 32, 55, 56, 60, 61, 64, 65, 66, 72, 73
Waltz, E. 11
Warhol, Andy 90
Weiglein, A.H. 104
Weinberg, P.D. 30
Weir, R.F. 56, 59, 62–63, 73
Weiss, G. 120, 124
Wendell, S. 81–82
Wilkinson, S. 18, 24, 39, 40–41, 42, 46–47
Winickoff, D.E. 68–69
Wolf, N. 87
World Health Organization (WHO) 31, 48–49

Yu, W. 31

Zhang, L. 35
Zimrin, A.B. 31